THE AMERICAN CIVIL WAR FOR YOUNG READERS

THE GREATEST BATTLES AND MOST HEROIC EVENTS OF THE AMERICAN CIVIL WAR

MARK BURTON

ISBN: 979-8-89095-005-5

CONTENTS

ATTENTION:

DO YOU WANT MY FUTURE BOOKS AT HEAVY DISCOUNTS AND EVEN FOR FREE?

HEAD OVER TO WWW.SECRETREADS.COM
AND JOIN MY SECRET BOOK CLUB!

INTRODUCTION

Why did an estimated 620,000 Americans choose to leave home to die in the Civil War between 1861 and 1865? These deaths outnumbered American deaths in all other wars fought by the United States from the start of the American Revolution in the late 1770s through to the Korean War in the early 1950s. Hundreds of thousands more Americans survived the Civil War after losing arms or legs shattered by bullets and cannonballs.

Why did roughly half of these war dead and so many of the wounded sacrifice themselves to defend the enslavement of human beings?

The Civil War is arguably the most significant event in the history of the United States. From the time of the American Revolution until the Civil War, Americans spoke of "these" United States, a country formed of separate states rather than one people. They often identified with their state. They called themselves Pennsylvanians or Mississippians, and so on, rather than Americans. The Civil War changed this. People in the United States now thought of themselves as Americans and described "the" United States as one nation.

In other words, the Civil War transformed the United States into the country we know today. No longer would people have stronger identities with their home state than the United States.

This newfound sense of unity was born from the moral question that started the war. How could a country that celebrated freedom continue to allow the enslavement of human beings? The Civil War answered that question by abolishing slavery.

In doing so, the war also ended the division between northern states that banned enslavement and southern states that defended the purchase of people. These were the two warring sides - the United States and a breakaway group of southern states calling themselves the Confederate States. The defeat of the Confederacy ended slavery.

The consequences of the Civil War still live with us. Defeating the rebellious supporters of enslavement was a significant victory on the road to creating a more perfect and unified United States. Abolishing enslavement was a moral victory.

But the war, due to the way it was fought and how it ended, left incomplete the issue of ensuring racial equality and economic opportunity for African Americans who had endured centuries of enslavement at the hands of white enslavers in the South. Most white southerners, whether they owned humans or not, continued to resist change. They surrendered the Confederacy, but they would not surrender white supremacy for another century.

It was the same for many white northerners. Despite efforts by some within the United States to integrate the races during the 1860s and 1870s, resistance proved too strong. This left deep wounds that refused to heal, wounds that reopened during more bloody battles for civil rights in the 20th century.

To understand the Civil War is to appreciate the cost of creating a more perfect nation and what it means to be American. The history of the Civil War helps us to understand today's debates about public statues honoring veterans of the war as well as to understand lingering injustices, all of which remain so rooted in the events of 1861 to 1865.

The smoke of battle cleared long ago, but the rumble of the guns continues to shake us.

WAR CLOUDS

FREE STATES   SLAVE STATES

"Crack!" The sound of the walking cane as it broke echoed through the Capitol and the country in May 1856.

Preston Brooks, a Representative from South Carolina, had crossed the halls of Congress to enter the chamber of the United States Senate. Once inside, he walked up to Charles Sumner, a famous abolitionist and Senator from Massachusetts. Brooks angrily disagreed with Sumner's position on slavery and then slammed his cane on Sumner's head to make his point. Brooks beat Sumner for several minutes before other Senators could stop the attack. The beating sent shockwaves across the nation.

Brooks, a pro-slavery politician, assaulted Sumner out of a twisted sense of honor. Sumner had given a speech condemning the enslavement of human beings as immoral. Brooks took offense.

He believed slavery was protected by the Bible and the Constitution. Millions of pro-slavery Americans, based largely in the slave-holding states south of the Ohio River, celebrated Brooks. Dozens of new canes were mailed to Brooks in the weeks after he assaulted Sumner.

The attack on Sumner left him unconscious. As he recovered, the voters of Sumner's home state of Massachusetts refused to replace the Senator, leaving his seat vacant in silent protest against pro-slavery politicians and in support of free speech. The people of Massachusetts even reelected Sumner later in 1856 despite his slow recovery. Sumner now suffered nightmares and headaches. After a failed attempt in 1857, he was finally able to return to his desk in the United States in 1859.

The violent attack by Brooks reflected the United States coming apart over the issue of slavery. For most of the country's history since independence in 1776, politicians had made uneasy compromises over the buying and selling of human beings.

White residents of southern states believed they required slavery to raise crops, such as cotton, sugar, and rice, on large plantations. White residents of northern states passed laws that slowly ended slavery in those states by the 1820s (though, in practice, it continued in some places until as late as 1850). These states focused on small family farms to raise crops like wheat and corn.

Both northern and southern states agreed that slavery west of the Mississippi River would be restricted under what was known as the Missouri Compromise of 1820. This agreement allowed Missouri to enter the United States as a pro-slavery state and Maine to enter the Union as a free state.

This maintained the balance of power between free states and slave states in the United States Senate, where each state had two Senators. This way, abolitionists could not pass laws restricting slavery everywhere in the country, and supporters of slavery could not pass laws making slavery legal across the country.

The Missouri Compromise also drew a line from the southern border of Missouri across the west to divide the remaining territory not yet formed into states. Territory to the north would be free states. Territory to the south would be slave states.

The Mexican-American War, beginning in 1846, ended the compromise. Southern states wanted the independent republic of Texas to join the United States as a slave state. This angered Mexico. Mexico's government saw Texas as part of Mexico despite the Texans' successful war for independence a decade earlier.

The attempt to turn Texas into a state of the United States provoked a war. Mexico lost. The United States forced Mexico, which had been badly defeated, to sign a treaty in 1848 that gave away roughly a third of its territory. This land contained the future states of California, Nevada, Arizona, Utah, and New Mexico.

The victory over Mexico shattered the compromise between free and slave states. The discovery of gold in California a year after the war ended led Congress to quickly bring it into the United States as a state out of fear that a foreign country might try to seize it. In the Compromise of 1850, California became a free state. This would end the even divide between free and slave states in the United States Senate.

To gain votes for California's statehood, pro-slavery politicians presented the Fugitive Slave Law. This law required that refugees from enslavement be returned to their owners even if the enslaved person lived in a northern state that prohibited slavery. Settlers in the territories taken from Mexico would vote on whether to allow slavery.

The Fugitive Slave Law angered many northerners. They refused to catch slaves. This anger grew louder after the publication of the novel *Uncle Tom's Cabin* by Harriet Beecher Stowe in 1852. Stowe, an abolitionist, told a story about Uncle Tom, an enslaved man in Kentucky, who was sent down the Mississippi River to the slave auctions in New Orleans. Uncle Tom died on the harsh cotton plantation run by Simon Legree. The violence faced by enslaved humans made many northerners angry and made the abolition of enslavement within the United States a common topic.

The debate over the future of slavery in the United States erupted into bloodshed in 1854. The Kansas-Nebraska Act passed by Congress allowed the territory of Kansas and Nebraska to become states, with local voters deciding whether to allow slavery or not, even though the areas would have been a 'free state' under the rules of the Missouri Compromise.

By organizing these areas and encouraging settlement, a railroad could be built that might stretch eventually to California, linking the gold-rich state to the rest of the Union.

The Act unleashed a wave of violent clashes in Kansas as it contained more residents and was closer to applying for statehood. Pro-slavery southerners encouraged settlers who agreed with their views to move to Kansas to increase the likelihood of Kansans voting for slavery. Abolitionist northerners did the same.

Henry Ward Beecher, a famous pastor in New York and brother of Harriet Beecher Stowe, urged his congregation to raise money for settlers opposed to slavery - and to purchase rifles for those already in Kansas so they could defend themselves from attacks by pro-slavery opponents. Shipments of rifles became known as "Beecher's Bibles."

The weapons were necessary as persons known as Border Ruffians, residents of neighboring Missouri who supported slavery, often rode into Kansas on horseback to scare away opponents.

Other abolitionists took steps to capture Americans' attention. William Lloyd Garrison, the publisher of the famous abolitionist newspaper *The Liberator*, founded in 1831, became notorious when, in Boston on July 4, 1854, he burned a copy of the United States Constitution to protest it as a pro-slavery document. Garrison showed in public what he had written several years earlier: "It matters not what is the theory of the government if the practice of the government be unjust and tyrannical." Garrison called for immediate justice and freedom for all.

Kansas quickly became known as "Bleeding Kansas" in the newspapers. The election of the territory's government in preparation for statehood led to a divided government. Kansas now had two capitals. One existed in Lawrence, Kansas, that opposed slavery. The other in Lecompton, Kansas, supported slavery.

In 1856, pro-slavery Kansans and Missourians raided Lawrence, destroying the local newspaper offices and burning several buildings. The abolitionist John Brown, who had traveled to Kansas to fight against slavery, responded to the attack on Lawrence by killing five settlers who supported the ownership of human beings. He then fled the territory as a man wanted for murder. Dozens of murders occurred in the following months as both sides attacked each other until federal officials established an uneasy peace in Kansas.

The fighting in Kansas and the attack on Charles Sumner by Preston Brooks made northern states and southern states increasingly suspicious of each other. Northern voters feared what they called the "Slave Power," the economic, social, and political influence of white southerners who backed the enslavement of people. White southern voters feared the growing support of abolitionism among northerners. This trend made white southerners more fearful given natural population growth.

Immigrants from Ireland and Germany, people who often opposed slavery, also flooded into northern cities during the 1830s, 1840s, and 1850s. This meant that pro-slavery southerners not only lost power in the United States Senate with California statehood, but they saw their power decline in the House of

Representatives too since representation in the House was linked to the population of each state.

Tempers became hotter when the United States Supreme Court intervened to define the issue of race and citizenship. In 1857, the Court announced its ruling in *Dred Scott v Sandford*. Scott, an enslaved African American born in the slave state of Virginia, had moved to Missouri after his enslavers relocated. Scott was then sold to an army officer who traveled into Wisconsin and other free states. Later, after returning to Missouri, Scott sued for his freedom 'on the grounds' that his time living in states where slavery was banned had made him free.

Chief Justice Roger Taney and his fellow Supreme Court justices disagreed with Scott. Taney argued that Scott, along with all African Americans in the United States, were not citizens under the Constitution and "can therefore claim none of the rights and privileges" granted to citizens because "whether emancipated or not" they remained under the power of the "dominant race," meaning whites. Taney's opinion was celebrated across the southern states where the enslavement of human beings thrived. Residents of northern states expressed horror.

The Supreme Court's ruling suggested that free states would soon need to allow slavery. More troubling, free African Americans living in northern states, even if they had never been enslaved, were second-class residents who, without a claim to citizenship, could easily find themselves kidnapped and forced into slavery.

Even before the Dred Scott decision, African Americans who had escaped enslavement wrote about the horrors of slavery and the fears of kidnapping.

Frederick Douglass in his *Narrative of the Life of Frederick Douglass* from 1845 told of how enslavers used fear to maintain slavery as a labor system. *Twelve Years a Slave*, written by Solomon Northup in 1853, described his kidnapping as a free man from New York. Invited to work in a high-paying job as a musician in Washington, D.C., he found himself held hostage and sent to the New Orleans slave market. After 12 years, Northrup managed to send word for help to relatives in New York who hired an attorney to secure his return to freedom and his family. Harriet Jacobs, in her *Incidents in the Life of a Slave Girl*, published in 1861, described a stressful seven years hiding in an attic in North Carolina to be near her enslaved children before making her escape to the North. Though beginning a life of freedom, she lived in terror of being discovered and returned to slavery.

Each of these books along with dozens of others from enslaved African Americans rallied public opinion against ownership of people even while white southerners loudly protested these books as exaggerations and lies.

As Americans argued over slavery, John Brown resurfaced. In the years since he fled Kansas, sympathetic abolitionists had helped Brown hide. They also funded his new plan to attack slavery.

In October 1859, Brown led a group of men to capture the federal armory in Harpers Ferry, Virginia. He hoped that the weapons stored there for the United States Army could be given away to the enslaved people in Virginia, sparking a war to end slavery. He expected the enslaved to flock to him. They would then head down southward along the Appalachian Mountains bringing freedom. Few enslaved people came. Locals, with aid from the Virginia militia and federal troops, quickly captured Brown and his group.

Brown was tried for treason against the state of Virginia and for attempting to cause a rebellion among the enslaved. He was hanged after giving his last written words: "I John Brown am now quite certain that the crimes of this guilty land will never be purged away, but with Blood."

The tensions over slavery and its future in the United States boiled over in the Presidential election of 1860. Could the political parties and their candidates fix the wounds of the country, maybe through more compromises that could ease the tensions? Or would the election worsen the divide separating slave states from free states? Would African Americans ever gain their citizenship rights after the Dred Scott decision? Would slavery spread into the northern states? Could the United States avoid civil war?

The 1860 election for president would be one of the most important in the history of the United States.

Did you know?

- The border between Maryland and Pennsylvania is known as the Mason-Dixon line, marking the divide between northern free states and southern slave states along the Atlantic coast.

- The Gold Rush in California in 1849 brought 300,000 people to California to dig for gold. These arrivals were known as '49ers.

- The slave states of the South were known as "Dixie" because the Citizens State Bank in New Orleans, the largest city within the region and major center of trade, issued a $10 note using the French word for ten – "dix."

- Harriet Beecher Stowe's *Uncle Tom's Cabin* was the best-selling novel of the 1850s. Stowe sold 300,000 copies in the first year of publication and two million copies worldwide by 1857.

- Many Irish immigrants fled to the United States to escape a severe famine resulting from a disease that killed potatoes in the late 1840s. Many German immigrants fled to the United States after a failed democratic revolution in Germany in 1848.

- The population of the United States in 1860 was 31 million people. Of these, nearly four million were enslaved African Americans.

ABRAHAM LINCOLN

"I believe this government cannot endure permanently half slave and half free," declared a man running for United States Senate from Illinois in 1858. That man was Abraham Lincoln.

Lincoln lost this election. But his speeches made him famous across the United States. He emerged as a rising star in a new political party called the Republican Party. Anti-slavery activists had then organized the Republican Party in 1854 to oppose the Kansas-Nebraska Act.

Lincoln had been born in 1809 in a small log cabin in Kentucky. His family moved a lot, heading soon to Indiana and then Illinois. Lincoln was nine years old when his mother died. The death left the family committed to working harder to survive life on the frontier.

Lincoln loved reading. By reading a wide range of books and newspapers, Lincoln taught himself about the world. He learned history, politics, religion, literature, and other topics. And he learned how to put words together into a convincing argument.

Lincoln worked a variety of jobs. One of the most important of these early jobs involved drifting a flatboat loaded with agricultural goods down the Mississippi River to the port of New Orleans. Flatboats used the current of the river to carry the boat downstream.

These journeys took about two weeks. After selling the goods, often pork and corn, carried onboard at New Orleans, Lincoln and the rest of the crew made the long walk upriver to return home. This journey lasted over a month or two.

For Lincoln, the slow trips gave him plenty of time to observe the large cotton and sugar plantations exploiting enslaved African Americans. Also, New Orleans contained the largest slave market in the United States. Auctions of human beings to the highest bidder often occurred. The experiences of these flatboat journeys showed Lincoln the cruelty of owning enslaved human beings for their labor.

Lincoln's interest in the law led him into politics. He won election to the state legislature of Illinois in 1834 and won re-election until he quit the legislature in 1842. During this time, he received permission from the Illinois court system to practice law too.

While practicing law and serving in elected office, Lincoln married. In 1839, Lincoln met Mary Todd, a native of Kentucky. He settled into a new life as a husband and a father. Lincoln and his wife welcomed the birth of their son Robert in 1843 and soon three other children over the next few years.

To care for this growing family, Lincoln settled into a career as a lawyer, leaving the legislature to be closer to his children and wife. He gained attention from the people around him for his ability to speak well, even though some people also thought his voice was too high-pitched.

In 1846, angered by the outbreak of war with Mexico, Lincoln briefly returned to politics. He won election to the United States Congress as a Representative. He served one term, leaving

Congress in 1849. Lincoln's re-engagement with politics occurred as the United States grew increasingly divided over the issue of slavery. Americans voiced particular concern over the expansion of slavery into new western territories such as Kansas and lands taken from Mexico at the end of the war.

Lincoln opposed any expansion of slavery outside of the states where ownership of human beings was already practiced. He was not an abolitionist. He was anti-slavery.

This meant he believed slavery should not expand into the western territories of the United States. He also believed that only allowing slavery in the southern states where ownership of human beings was already permitted would slowly end the practice there as these states developed more industry, becoming more like the economy of the northern states.

Angry over events in Kansas, in 1858 Lincoln again restarted his political career to challenge Stephen Douglas, the Democrat from Illinois who had written the Kansas-Nebraska Act. Both men campaigned to represent Illinois in the United States Senate.

Lincoln had joined the new Republican Party. Formed in 1854, the Republican Party strongly opposed the spread of slavery into the western territories of the United States. Lincoln lost the election. But his speeches in several debates with Stephens held in towns across Illinois brought Lincoln national recognition. He became a rising star of the Republican Party.

This recognition resulted in a rematch of Lincoln and Douglas in 1860 for a much more important political job - President of the United States. The Republican Party in 1860 selected Lincoln because he was seen as more moderate on the issue of ending slavery than the other leading politician within the Party. That man was the governor of New York named William Seward. Republicans believed that a more moderate candidate would win more votes in northern states where many white voters remained uncertain about the abolition of slavery in the United States. Many white voters feared the end of slavery could lead to an acceptance of racial equality.

Douglas gained the nomination of the Democratic Party. He tried to avoid the argument over slavery by supporting the idea of "popular sovereignty." As in the Kansas-Nebraska Act, popular sovereignty meant letting voters within a new territory applying for statehood decide whether to permit slavery or not.

Douglas's proposal of allowing popular sovereignty angered many northerners who opposed any possibility of expanding slavery westward, a ban established in the Missouri Compromise.

These northerners also feared that the idea of popular sovereignty opened the door to northern states allowing slavery despite their long history of being free states. This was a real worry, especially after the Supreme Court's Dred Scott decision suggested that slavery should be legal throughout the United States.

Douglas's idea also angered many southerners. They increasingly believed that slavery should be permitted everywhere in the United States. After Douglas won the nomination at the Democratic Party convention in Charleston, South Carolina, party members from southern states left the party to hold another convention in Baltimore, Maryland. These Democrats nominated for President the current Vice-President; a man named John C. Breckinridge of Kentucky. Breckinridge was a strong supporter of slavery. The Democratic Party now had two Presidential candidates.

A few southerners, afraid that the nation was dangerously divided over slavery, organized a more moderate Constitutional Union Party and nominated John Bell of Tennessee.

This party received most of its support from states known as the "Upper South," slave states that bordered the northern free states and would be on the front line of any war. Supporters of the Constitutional Union Party argued that love of the Constitution was the most important issue.

They tried to ignore the debate over slavery in order to save the nation.

The election of 1860 was actually two races. In the free North, Lincoln competed with Douglas. Lincoln swept all these states. In the slave South, Breckinridge competed with Bell, winning most of these states.

Overall, Lincoln's win in the northern free states where most Americans lived meant that he had won the election. The United States Constitution orders that the president is elected by the Electoral College in which each state is given a number based on how many people live in it.

When a candidate won a state, the candidate received all that state's electors. In 1860, Lincoln collected 180 Electoral College votes. His three opponents only totaled a combined 123 Electoral College votes.

Lincoln had become President of the United States. Pro-slavery southerners were scared that they had lost their influence over the federal government. They feared what this might mean for their hold on human beings as property.

Did you know?

- Lincoln is the tallest president in United States history. He stood 6 feet, 4 inches tall.

- Lincoln's favorite food was apples.

- A flatboat in the 1830s took about 12 days to travel the distance from Cincinnati, Ohio, to New Orleans, Louisiana. This distance was 1,560 miles with a speed of around five miles per hour.

- Abraham Lincoln grew a beard after receiving a letter from Grace Bedell, an 11-year-old from Westfield, New York. Bedell, sending the letter a few weeks before election day in 1860, suggested the beard would help Lincoln's chance of winning the Presidency. Lincoln kept the beard until his death.

- Lincoln won the Presidency in 1860 with 59% of the votes in the Electoral College, but he received less than 40% of the popular vote, meaning all the votes cast by Americans in the election.

- Although born in Kentucky, Lincoln's opposition to slavery made him very unpopular. He received only 1,364 votes in his home state. This was less than 1% of the 146,216 votes cast in Kentucky during the 1860 Presidential election.

THE CONFEDERATE GOVERNMENT

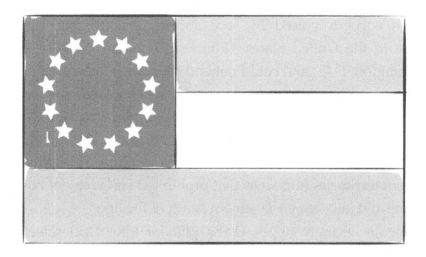

"In your hands, my dissatisfied fellow-countrymen, and not in mine, is the momentous issue of civil war," stated Lincoln in his inaugural address in March 1861. He had attempted to reassure residents of the southern states who supported slavery that he would not interfere with the practice where it existed. But Lincoln already knew that several slave states had abandoned the United States to create a new country. He feared more might follow.

The time between Lincoln's election in November 1860 and his inauguration in March 1861 has become known as the Secession Crisis, as pro-slavery southern states departed or threatened to depart the United States. Some Americans, in the North and South, looked to avoid a breakup by offering compromises.

One of the most popular proposals was the Crittenden Compromise. John Crittenden, a United States Senator from Kentucky, offered a range of new amendments to the Constitution to protect the enslavement of people.

Each amendment under the Crittenden Compromise aimed to ease a concern voiced by secessionists, encouraging them to return to the United States. Congress could not ban slavery in Washington, D.C., and could not end the trade of enslaved people across state lines. Congress also could not ban slavery on federal property, like forts, in states where enslavement was legal. To ease concerns among northerners in the free states, an amendment proposed restoring the Missouri Compromise line dividing western territories into areas that prohibited enslavement north of the line and allowed enslavement south of the line.

Lincoln strongly opposed the plan of John Crittenden. The plan failed.

Angry pro-slavery southerners feared what an anti-slavery president like Abraham Lincoln might do to restrict the ownership and sale of human beings. As president, Lincoln had the power to appoint postmasters at post offices across the United States. He could also appoint customs collectors responsible for taxing exports and imports at the ports. Would Lincoln appoint anti-slavery supporters, or even outright abolitionists, to these positions? These were serious concerns for supporters of slavery.

For decades pro-slavery southerners had exercised their political power in Congress to pressure presidents to appoint postmasters to the southern states who supported slavery. These postmasters threw away leaflets, newspapers, and other mail sent by abolitionists calling for the end of enslavement, thereby undermining opposition to slavery among white southerners and preventing possible rebellion by the enslaved.

Plus, the president nominated Supreme Court Justices, diplomats to foreign countries, and other positions in the federal government. He could also veto laws passed by Congress that might protect slavery. This was too much to risk for pro-slavery southerners, especially those with millions of dollars invested in human beings as property.

Many pro-slavery southerners believed the best solution to protect slavery was to leave the United States and create a new country. Removing a state from the United States was called secession, and supporters of the idea were called secessionists.

No southern state was more vocal in advocating for secession than the people of South Carolina. The governor and state legislature called a convention to discuss the issue. On December 20, 1860, delegates to the convention voted to secede. South Carolina's actions inspired other southern states to follow. In January 1861, Mississippi, Florida, Alabama, Georgia, and Louisiana left the United States. In February, Texas seceded.

Secessionists from these states agreed to meet in Montgomery, Alabama, to organize a new national government they called the Confederate States of America. They aimed to draft a new constitution that strengthened the protections of slavery. They copied much of the United States Constitution, but the slight differences are worth recognizing.

The introduction to the United States Constitution called the Preamble, stated, "We the People of the United States, in Order to form a more perfect Union, establish Justice, insure domestic Tranquility, provide for the common defence, promote the general Welfare, and secure the Blessings of Liberty to ourselves and our Posterity, do ordain and establish this Constitution for the United States of America."

The secessionists in Montgomery started the Confederacy's constitution with different words: "We, the people of the Confederate States, each state acting in its sovereign and independent character, in order to form a permanent federal government, establish justice, insure domestic tranquility, and secure the blessing of liberty to ourselves and our posterity - invoking the favor and guidance of Almighty God - do ordain and establish this Constitution for the Confederate States of America." Elsewhere in the document, the secessionists included the word "slaves" and "slaveholding," words the founders of the United States refused to use given that some opposed enslavement of people.

The creators of the Confederacy believed in a principle called states' rights. This view held that states, as the Confederate preamble says, are sovereign and independent, meaning power rested with the state government rather than the people. No mention is made of creating a Union because that was not the goal. The Confederate government was largely empowered to focus on the defense of the new nation and on negotiating with foreign countries. Within the Confederacy, states remained supreme.

The Confederate constitution had other differences. It ordered that the president be elected to only one six-year term, rather than the four-year term of the President of the United States who could be re-elected for more terms. Confederate politicians faced more restrictions on raising money for the new national government.

The Confederate constitution also allowed states to impeach, meaning remove, Confederate officials they opposed if the state legislature where that official worked and lived passed impeachment by a two-thirds vote. Writers of this constitution wanted a weak national government. They wanted to ensure that states joining the Confederacy would not find themselves under a national government that could interfere too much with life in the member states. The fears that arose from membership in the United States would not be an issue in the Confederate States.

The supremacy of the states was reflected in how the convention selected a provisional, meaning temporary, Confederate president, vice-president, and cabinet to manage the government. A congress was also established. Delegates chose Jefferson Davis of Mississippi, a veteran of the Mexican-American War and a United States Senator who had briefly served as Secretary of War during the 1850s, as the Confederacy's first president. Other major positions were divided among the

Confederate states. A man from South Carolina became Treasurer. A Texan served as Postmaster. The post of Attorney General went to a Louisianan. A Georgian accepted the position of Secretary of State while an Alabaman worked as Secretary of War.

The Montgomery delegates did not create a supreme court because of fears that such a court could rule against states if those states disagreed with laws passed by the Confederate Congress or rules made by the Confederate president. The provisional government creating the Confederacy became permanent after elections held in November 1861.

Of course, the key issue protected by the states' rights principle was each state's right to protect the practice of enslaving and trading people. The issue of states' rights and slavery were firmly bound together in the Confederacy.

No one made this point clearer than Alexander H. Stephens, a lifelong politician from Georgia who was selected as the Vice-President of the Confederacy while attending the convention in Montgomery. In a speech given in Savannah, Georgia, in March 1861, Stephens rallied support for the new Confederate government. He did so while also criticizing the United States Constitution for being based "upon the assumption of the equality of races." This was "an error" in his view. White supremacy rested at the heart of the Confederate cause. The Confederate government's "foundations are laid, its cornerstone rests, upon the great truth" that enslaved African Americans were "not equal to the white man; that slavery subordination to the superior race is his natural and normal condition."

Racism formed the core of the Confederate effort.

Secessionists also believed they enslaved people as a Christian duty. Note that the preamble to the Confederate constitution makes a direct reference to "invoking the favor and guidance of

Almighty God." Supporters of the enslavement of African Americans convinced themselves that the Bible supported slavery. Pressed by northern abolitionists who condemned slavery as immoral and dehumanizing, pro-slavery southerners since the 1830s had responded by combing the Bible for any references to support their labor system.

Defenders of slavery pointed to the existence of slavery in the Old Testament. They also referenced the so-called Curse of Ham, a story in the Bible about Noah's punishment of a son. Pro-slavery pastors claimed this punishment fell on descendants of the son who had moved to Africa. In their telling, dark skin color marked those who should be enslaved even though the Bible makes no mention of skin tone.

Pro-slavery southerners also argued that their Christian duty required them to care for African Americans, who they saw as inferior. Enslavers emphasized Bible passages that told the enslaved to obey their owners. White southerners considered themselves like parents and enslaved African Americans like children.

The fact that enslavers refused to educate the human beings they owned or to give them many opportunities outside of the cotton, sugar, and rice fields did not matter. The lack of education, especially restrictions on teaching the enslaved the ability to read or write, kept enslaved African Americans from organizing resistance or escaping. This refusal to provide education reinforced enslavers' views that the human beings they owned were not intelligent enough to care for themselves.

Supporters of the Confederacy believed that they would peacefully leave the United States. Many doubted Lincoln would attempt to bring the Confederate states back into the Union. But they did hope that Upper South slave states that had not seceded

- Maryland, Virginia, North Carolina, Kentucky, Tennessee, Arkansas, and Missouri - might apply to the Confederacy if Lincoln threatened to attack. Most people in these Upper South states wanted to remain loyal to the United States but, as states that supported enslavement of African Americans, they did not want to see Lincoln invade the Confederacy.

Finally, Confederates felt confident that they would be successful in establishing their new nation because they believed in the power of cotton, the South's main crop. Mills in Great Britain and France relied on the South's cotton crop to produce cheap clothes sold on the world market. These mills were a major industry in both countries. Confederates thought that the loss of their cotton supply would cause the mills to close, resulting in high unemployment in Great Britain and France that might lead to protests and riots. This foreign policy was known as "cotton diplomacy."

In the secessionists' view, British and French political leaders would soon recognize the Confederate States of America as a new nation. Doing so would lead to stronger trade ties with Europe. Most importantly, though, recognition of the Confederacy by foreign countries meant access to aid in the form of loans and weapons should President Lincoln attempt to interfere with secessionists' plans.

With the Confederate government established, secessionists now waited to see what Lincoln would do after taking the Presidential oath of office in March 1861.

Did you know?

- Historians call the years before the Civil War, roughly from 1820 until 1860, the "antebellum period." The word "antebellum" is a Latin word meaning "before war."

- In the decade before secession, white southerners were so convinced of the global importance of cotton that they used the phrase "King Cotton" when talking about the crop.

- Outspoken secessionists were criticized as "fire-eaters" during the 1850s. The term cast them as extremists.

- To reach Washington, D.C., for his inauguration, Lincoln had to disguise himself to sneak through Baltimore, Maryland, where rumors circulated about Confederate sympathizers plotting to assassinate him.

- The official seal of the Confederate States of America featured an image of George Washington, the first President of the United States. Confederates believed they were preserving the ideals of the American Revolution.

- Delaware did not secede even though it allowed the enslavement of African Americans. It was the only slave state where no fighting occurred during the Civil War.

FORT SUMTER

On a small island in the center of the harbor at Charleston, South Carolina, sat Fort Sumter. The fort formed part of a network of brick fortifications placed near the most important ports of the United States to protect them from attack by foreign countries. Now the attack threatened to come from onshore as Confederate soldiers aimed their weapons at the tall brick walls.

Across the Confederacy, supporters of the new country rushed to seize the federal armories for their stockpiles of ammunition and weapons. Confederate troops also marched toward the federal forts to capture these large structures manned by small, isolated units of United States soldiers.

Forts with easy access by land were quick to fall. Outside Savannah, Georgia, locals captured Fort Pulaski. Near New Orleans, Louisiana, Confederate forces seized Fort Jackson and Fort St. Philip, among several smaller forts scattered along the waterways surrounding the city.

Confederate officials feared that delay would risk Lincoln sending reinforcements and using the forts to cut off trade to southern ports. But some forts, especially those surrounded largely by water, proved more difficult to take.

President Lincoln rushed reinforcements to Fort Monroe in Virginia shortly after taking office and before Virginia voted on secession. The fort was located on a strip of land with water on three sides. Defense of the fort was easy because most members of the United States Navy remained loyal rather than leaving to join the Confederate Navy.

One fort along the coast of the Confederacy troubled Lincoln the most, Fort Sumter.

Upon hearing of South Carolina's decision to secede in December 1860, Major Robert Anderson of the United States Army ordered the immediate evacuation of forts on the mainland near Charleston. He burned supplies left behind and spiked the cannons, meaning he clogged their barrels to make them unusable. Major Anderson retreated to the imposing Fort Sumter surrounded by the waters of the Atlantic Ocean.

The governor of South Carolina ordered Major Anderson to surrender. The army officer refused. An attempt to resupply the fort in January 1861 led cadets at a local military college called The Citadel to fire cannons at the ship *Star of the West*, forcing it away before it could reach Fort Sumter. The cannon blasts were the first shots of what would become the Civil War, though southerners and northerners still hoped to avoid bloodshed. The first Confederate commander, General P.G.T. Beauregard, was ordered to Charleston to coordinate the military effort, and he also demanded that Major Anderson surrender. Again, the officer refused.

By the time Lincoln took office in March 1861, the defiant Major Anderson and his soldiers were running low on food and other supplies. The President wanted to avoid a confrontation that might worsen the secession crisis by causing more states to leave the Union. He also did not want to harden the position of Confederate states. Lincoln hoped he might convince the seceded states to return to the United States. But time was running out. Lincoln had to rescue the brave soldiers holding out in Fort Sumter. He ordered a fleet of warships to head to Charleston.

The first ship sent by Lincoln came into view of Charleston on April 11, 1861. Confederate Gen. Beauregard now knew that he too was out of time. If he failed to capture Fort Sumter before all of the US' fleet arrived, the Confederate Army had no possibility of seizing Fort Sumter. The cannons on the ships and the resupplied fort would also threaten Charleston.

At 4:30 a.m. on April 12, 1861, the Confederate cannons began blasting Fort Sumter. For the next 34 hours, shells from the batteries rained down upon Maj. Anderson and his command of over a hundred soldiers. The thunder of the big guns woke residents of Charleston. Many lined the shoreline to watch the bombardment as dawn broke over the harbor.

The pummeling rattled Fort Sumter as well as the nerves of the soldiers inside. Major Anderson agreed to surrender but on the condition that he and his men return to the United States along with the American flag that flew over the fort. He could also fire the fort's cannons in a 100-round salute to the flag.

Until the attack on Fort Sumter, some Americans in the North and the South had hoped to avoid war. News of the bombardment of Fort Sumter convinced Americans in the United States that war was now unavoidable.

On April 15, 1861, President Lincoln called for 75,000 volunteers to defend the United States and to end what he considered a rebellion against the nation. Many more than that number rallied to the muster stations to take up arms. The units they formed became known as the "Federal" or "Union" forces. To them, their southern opponents were rebels or "secesh."

News of Lincoln's enlistment of so many volunteers convinced Americans in the Confederate States that war was inevitable. A wave of white southerners rushed to enlist to defend their new country and, even more important for many of these recruits, their home state. These Confederates called their opponents "Yanks," short for Yankee.

Lincoln's effort to raise an army sent shockwaves through the Upper South. War threatened slavery by disrupting routines, drawing away local white men, and giving enslaved African

Americans opportunities to undermine the society built upon their backs. This concern led pro-slavery states initially reluctant to join the Confederacy to leap out of the United States.

Virginia seceded two days after Fort Sumter surrendered. In May, Arkansas and North Carolina abandoned the United States. In June, Tennessee left. The Confederate States of America now contained 11 states.

In Missouri, the state governor and some legislators voted to secede. Enslavers maintained a wealthy line of cotton plantations along the Missouri River in the center of the state and along the Mississippi River. But many other Missourians, especially those in the large city of St. Louis, opposed the move. Missouri was deadlocked. Deadly violence soon erupted as small groups of men clashed over the issue. Some of the most vicious, brutal fighting of the coming Civil War occurred in Missouri.

In Kentucky, a group of secessionists created a new state government when the largely pro-Union legislature refused to consider leaving the United States. A slave state, Kentucky contained a population of wealthy enslavers who focused on growing tobacco. The climate of Kentucky was less suited to cotton. Roughly a third of Kentuckians supported the Confederacy.

The division of opinion on secession splitting Kentucky and Missouri kept them in the Union.

A similar division of opinion split some Upper South states that joined the Confederacy after Fort Sumter surrendered. In eastern Tennessee, a mountainous area along the Appalachians, pro-Union sentiment was strong. Many of these Tennesseans resisted the Confederacy.

In western Virginia, an isolated area along the Appalachian Mountains, people also opposed the state's secession. This area was linked by trade to the Ohio River, making commerce with the free northern states vital to the local economy.

Also, the rocky land of western Virginia was not suited to large plantations with enslaved African American laborers. Small family farms dotted the hills. Opponents of secession took steps for the western counties to secede from Virginia. In June 1863, these counties would be recognized as a new member of the United States called West Virginia.

Did you know?

- Fort Sumter and other brick forts outside American ports were built after the War of 1812, a conflict fought between Great Britain and the United States.

- Fort Sumter was built on a man-made island started in 1829. The island placed the fort in the center of the harbor, making it easy to fire on any attacking ships.

- The only soldier to die at Fort Sumter - and the first death of the Civil War - was Private Daniel Hough. He died when ammunition loaded into a cannon during the 100-round salute to the American flag exploded before the gun crew was ready.

- Captain Abner Doubleday received the honor of firing the first shot in defense of the United States when he lit the fuse on one of Fort Sumter's cannons. Doubleday is even more famous for inventing baseball in 1839 on a cow pasture outside Cooperstown, New York.

- Major Robert Anderson took the American flag that flew over Fort Sumter to New York, where it soon fluttered over a statue of President George Washington in Union Square. A crowd of over 100,000 went to see the flag raised, believed by some historians to be the largest gathering of Americans in the history of the United States up to that time.

- Residents of Charleston still call the shoreline where Confederates placed artillery, The Battery.

BULL RUN

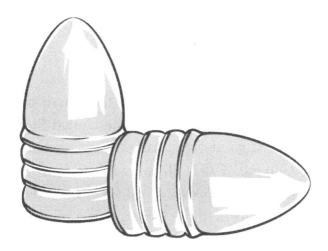

Mary Chesnutt, the wife of a Confederate official who worked closely with President Jefferson Davis, wrote in her diary after the first major battle of the Civil War at Bull Run Creek in Virginia on July 21, 1861. Barely 30 miles away from Washington, D.C., the fight awakened Americans to the damage the war would cause.

Chesnutt recorded, "Witnessed for the first time a military funeral. As the march came wailing up, they say (a family friend named) Mrs. Bartow fainted." The procession of the horse-drawn carriage carrying the coffin of Colonel Francis Bartow stuck in Chesnutt's memory. She penned, "The empty saddle and the led war-horse - we saw and heard it all; and now it seems we are never out of the sound of the Dead March."

In the aftermath of Fort Sumter, Lincoln's call to arms brought thousands into the United States Army. He needed troops. The peacetime army was scattered mostly along the western frontier in various forts. Patrolling on horseback, these soldiers guarded against attacks by Native Americans - nations like the Sioux, Pawnee, and Comanche. These people resisted settlers from the United States who encroached on their lands.

In December 1860, the United States only had 16,000 troops. Many of the officers and soldiers in this small army, despite taking oaths of allegiance to defend the United States, deserted to join the new Confederate Army. These included men like Confederate Generals P.G.T. Beauregard, Robert E. Lee, Albert Sidney Johnston, and dozens of others. These deserters were some of the best officers in the United States military, giving the Confederacy an important advantage on future battlefields.

To subdue the Confederacy and restore the seceded states to the Union, Lincoln needed to rebuild the United States Army into an effective fighting force. But first, he needed to ensure the safety of Washington, D.C. He rushed troops to protect the Capitol because the District of Columbia sat wedged between the slave states of Maryland and Virginia. Although Maryland did not secede, the state contained many Confederate sympathizers.

Plus, Lincoln could look out of the White House window to see the hills of Virginia across the Potomac River. And thousands of Confederate troops were concentrating in northern Virginia, not far away.

The Confederate government established in Montgomery agreed to move the capital of the Confederacy from Alabama to

Richmond, Virginia, in appreciation for that state's secession from the United States. Given that the American Revolution was won at Yorktown, Virginia, in 1781, the state had symbolic importance for all Americans. That Virginia joined the Confederacy reinforced secessionists' belief that they were restoring the ideals of the Revolution, not destroying those ideals. Barely a hundred miles separated the capital of the United States and the capital of the Confederate States.

Lincoln's call for volunteers to preserve the Union inspired thousands of southerners to enlist in the Confederate Army to defend the new country from any possible invasion. Units rushed to Virginia to protect Richmond. A soldier from North Carolina described the railroad ride northward in April 1861: "Our trip was full of joy and pleasure, for at every station where our train stopped the ladies showered us with flowers." His unit, the First North Carolina Regiment, received a warm welcome when the troops stepped from the train to march to their final destination. The North Carolinian wrote, "The streets were lined with people, cheering us."

Confederate generals moved troops to Bull Run Creek because the stream was easy to defend. From their positions, the rebel soldiers blocked any invasion by the Federals gathering in Washington, D.C.

Once Lincoln felt he had enough troops, he decided that he could no longer wait. The President felt intense pressure. Newspapers across the United States called for action. Congress too pushed Lincoln to show resolve. He needed to crush the rebels along Bull Run Creek and restore the Union.

Northerners and southerners believed that the war would be fun. They also believed the war would be short, with the first battle easily defeating the other side. Officials were so convinced of this that enlistment contracts for the first wave of volunteers only required them to serve for 90 days.

So, Lincoln had a problem. Having called for volunteers after the fall of Fort Sumter in late April 1861, the first men to enlist were soon to reach the end of their enlistment contracts by late July 1861. If he didn't use these troops who'd joined expecting the adventure of a battle, these men might refuse to reenlist, preferring to head back home. Lincoln was running out of time.

Lincoln ordered General Irwin McDowell, who over the summer had hurriedly trained and organized the 35,000 troops in Washington, D.C., to move out on July 16, 1861. McDowell's force was the largest army so far ever assembled in the United States. His army confronted a line of Confederate troops numbering around 32,000 under the command of General P.G.T. Beauregard and General Joseph Johnston.

Residents of Washington, D.C., were so confident of McDowell's victory that several hundred civilians rode their carriages to the hillsides overlooking Bull Run Creek to watch the battle. Men, women, and children enjoyed picnics spread onto blankets. They peered at the fields through binoculars. Among these observers were several prominent members of Congress, men who had urged Lincoln to order the offensive.

McDowell maneuvered his troops across weakly defended parts of Bull Run Creek to the hills beyond, then turned toward the main rebel army. The Confederate brigades rushed to confront the Federal troops.

Through the thick smoke of battle, lines of soldiers faced off. A hundred or so yards apart, these units fired musket and rifle fire into each other. Volley after volley tore flesh and shattered bones. Cannon shot and shells ripped holes in the formations. The excitement and anticipation these young men felt as they approached Bull Run Creek on what they believed to be the adventure of a lifetime quickly turned into terror and horror. Friends and comrades fell, wounded or dead. Large pools of blood soaked the ground. Broken bodies piled up.

The Confederate and Federal battlelines bent under pressure. They regrouped. Fought harder. And then, exhausted, the Federal soldiers broke and ran as fresh Confederate reinforcements arrived on the field. The rebels had proven they would not be easily conquered.

McDowell's army collapsed into a rout. Regiments disintegrated. Even whole brigades evaporated. Equipment thrown way by fleeing soldiers clogged the roads - firearms, knapsacks, and anything else that slowed the men down. Civilians who had enjoyed a picnic while expecting a Union victory fled in fear too. They rushed onto their carriages for the ride back to Washington, D.C., making the chaos on the roads even worse.

The Confederates - those still alive and unwounded - were too fatigued to chase McDowell's retreating army. An important battle had been won. Victory in the war would have to wait.

Both sides realized that the war would not end soon. Soldiers with expiring 90-day enlistments signed up for years of service. The victory at Bull Run inspired more southerners to join the Confederate Army to finish the job of winning independence for their new country. The defeat toughened the resolve of Americans in the United States too. They were determined to restore the Union and furious at the thought that the Confederacy might achieve secession so quickly.

One young man in Pennsylvania, like tens of thousands of others, wrote in his diary in September 1861: "Exchanged home and friends and all that was near and dear to me, for camp life, and left home, with a final farewell, for the seat of war."

Did you know?

- Confederates usually named battles after the nearest town or land feature. They called the struggle along Bull Run Creek by the name Battle of Manassas, for a railroad depot close to the battle. They also often named their armies after land areas, such as the Army of Northern Virginia or the Army of Tennessee.

- Federals usually named battles after the nearest waterway. They also regularly named their armies after waterways, such as the Army of the Potomac or the Army of the Tennessee.

- Federals wore blue uniforms. Confederates wore gray uniforms. Later in the war, as cloth and dye supplies dwindled, Confederates bleached captured Union blue uniforms and other fabric in a mixture of crushed nut shells. The resulting tan color was called butternut, the most widespread color of Confederate uniforms by 1864.

- The flag of the United States was called the Stars and Stripes. The flag of the Confederacy was called the Stars and Bars.

- Bullets used during the Civil War were called Minié balls. A Frenchman named Claude-Étienne Minié invented bullets with a hollow base in 1847. When firing a rifle, the hollow base expanded into the ridged lining, called rifling, in the muzzle of a musket. The resulting spin of the bullet made the shot go farther with more accuracy.

- The three main branches of service within Civil War armies were infantry, artillery, and cavalry. Uniforms of both the Federals and Confederates were color coded with trim to identify a soldier's branch. These were blue for infantry, red for artillery, and yellow for cavalry.

ANACONDA PLAN

The defeat at Bull Run brought a realization to President Lincoln and his generals that the war would be a prolonged affair. They saw no easy victory ahead. Thankfully, a plan designed by General Winfield Scott guided the United States during the next bloody four years of warfare.

Scott explained the plan in simple language in May 1861: "We rely greatly on the sure operation of a complete blockade of the Atlantic and Gulf ports soon to commence. In connection with such blockade, we propose a powerful movement down the Mississippi [River] to the ocean, with a cordon of posts at proper points." The strategy became known as the Anaconda Plan.

Scott had plenty of experience. He was 75 years old when the Battle of Bull Run occurred - far too old to direct long campaigns while riding horseback. Scott started his military career as a captain of artillery way back in 1808. He fought in several battles during the War of 1812. Most famously, in 1847, Scott led a large amphibious landing at Vera Cruz, Mexico, during the Mexican-American War. His column of troops marched inland and captured Mexico City, ending the war.

Scott understood the difficulties of marching large armies across vast stretches of land. He grasped the complexities of positioning navies and coordinating the movement of ships and troops. Most importantly, the general, nicknamed "Old Fuss and Feathers" for his attention to detail, knew how to defeat a country the size of the Confederacy.

The 11 states of the Confederacy contained 5.5 million free people, almost all white, and 3.5 million enslaved people, mostly African Americans but also very few Africans. Money held in banks along with coined money in circulation amounted to $74 million. The Confederacy also claimed 35 million head of livestock. Its 21,000 factories were linked by 9,000 miles of railroad tracks. Mostly, though, the southern economy rested firmly upon cotton fields. Roughly 69% of southerners worked as farmers. All of this lay scattered across roughly 750,000 square miles.

Scott could easily see the advantages held by the United States. With a population of 18.5 million, the military could recruit from a far larger pool of men. Banks and coined money amounted to $234 million. A prolonged war was more affordable to them. The Union contained 40 million head of livestock. Significantly, the United States possessed 3.4 million horses compared to the Confederacy's 1.7 million horses. Horses were vital to pull cannons, move supply wagons, and equipping cavalry.

Although still heavily agricultural, the United States' greatest strength was a rapidly growing industrial economy. Some 101,000 factories hummed in the North, sending products onto a network of 20,000 miles of railroad track. These factories would now expand to produce artillery, rifles, ammunition, uniforms, and all the other equipment needed to fight a war. The diverse economy meant that only 48% of Americans in the United States worked as farmers.

Lincoln argued that secessionists had launched a rebellion not only against the United States Constitution but also against their state governments. The Constitution required the President to "guarantee to every State in this Union a Republican Form of Government." Lincoln refused to recognize the Confederacy as a separate nation. Instead, the United States had fallen into civil war, a conflict within the United States between lawfully elected representatives and a group of outlaws in rebellion. Some northerners even termed the conflict "The Great Rebellion" or "The War for the Union."

How then would Scott's plan guide Lincoln in his effort to smash this rebellion?

Scott instructed that the United States Navy blockade the Confederacy's ports. This bottled up the region's cotton and other crops, preventing these goods from being sold to European countries. The sale of cotton was the Confederacy's chief means of raising money for its war effort.

The blockade also isolated the Confederacy from supplies it desperately needed. With an economy so focused on agriculture, especially cotton, the rebelling southerners lacked enough industries to manufacture the cannons, rifles, medicines, uniforms, and other equipment required to fight a war. To supply armies and sustain the southern population, the Confederates needed imports of European manufactured goods. This was not a major issue in 1861 or 1862 when shelves and warehouses were full after seizures of federal forts and arsenals stockpiled with supplies. But as the war raged over the years, the blockade strangled the Confederacy.

Scott's Anaconda Plan, named for the large snake that slowly strangles its prey before swallowing it whole, would choke the Confederacy, so the armies of the United States could demolish the weakened rebel military.

Scott's idea took time. The Confederacy covered a large chunk of the North American continent. Although many northerners believed, through 1861, that a quick victory might still be gained with some luck and some incredible courage in a major battle, the long lists of dead and wounded from places like Bull Run increasingly showed that this belief was foolish. But a blockade of the Confederacy seemed equally ambitious. Some 3,500 miles of coastline needed to be sealed off from the rest of the world. This stretched from Washington, D.C., down to Brownsville, Texas, on the border with Mexico.

For Scott's plan to work, the United States needed two things: ships and bases. Sailors largely remained loyal to the US Navy. Very few deserted to the Confederacy's nearly non-existent fleet.

But the Union fleet was small for the task now assigned to it by Scott. In early 1861, the US Navy had 90 warships on the books manned by barely 9,000 sailors. Only 42 of these vessels were in active service. The rest of the fleet was unfit for the high seas. Worse, many of the 42 operational ships were stationed far overseas guarding American interests.

The United States' factories and shipyards focused on the task of launching the extra ships needed to make Scott's strategy successful. By the end of 1861, the US Navy numbered over 250 ships. A year later, the US Navy expanded to over 450 vessels. By 1863, the military finally had enough ships to make the blockade very effective. Still, more ships were launched to tighten the stranglehold. When the war ended in early 1865, the US Navy contained 626 warships operated by roughly 59,000 sailors, the largest fleet in the world.

Lacking much industry, the Confederacy could barely counterattack with the few ships built within its borders. Plastered with sheets of iron, these ironclads challenged the blockading US Navy built with so much exposed wood, making them vulnerable. But the Confederate ironclads were few in number and soon the US Navy manufactured its own ironclads to confront the rebels.

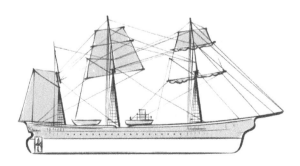

The Confederacy also arranged for shipyards in Great Britain to construct a handful of fast ocean-going warships called commerce raiders. These vessels were designed to attack merchant ships sailing from ports in the United States, disrupting trade. Equipped with only a few cannons, commerce raiders generally avoided Federal warships.

Scott's plan also called for bases. The Union strategy looked to capture parts of the Confederate coastline to provide a base of operations that could support the fleet offshore. These bases served double duty. They stored supplies, like water, food, and parts, needed by the US Navy to stay in action far from the shipyards in Boston, New York, or elsewhere in the North.

The bases also allowed the US army to harass Confederate forces, drawing southern soldiers away from the battlefront. Federal generals would use these bases to order troops on raids into the surrounding countryside. These troops captured goods, destroyed infrastructure, and encouraged the enslaved to abandon the plantations.

Mixed into Scott's plan was the construction of several dozen warships designed to patrol rivers. Scott not only aimed to seal the Confederacy's coastline. His Anaconda Plan specifically called for controlling the Mississippi River. Ironclads sailing downriver from the North into the Confederacy strangled the South by preventing the transportation of men and supplies across waterways, complicating the rebels' efforts to wage war.

Equally important, capturing all of the Mississippi River allowed fast shipments of supplies to the US Navy ships blockading the Gulf Coast. Without access to the Mississippi River, supplies needed to go all the way around Florida to reach the Gulf of Mexico.

To counter this part of the Anaconda Plan, the Confederacy built forts equipped with large-caliber artillery along its navigable rivers. These forts became key objectives for the Federal Army to capture to give the Union fleet free access to the waterways.

General Scott retired late in 1861. He was too old, too heavy, and too ill to manage the war. The conflict called for younger generals with more energy, though far less experience, to execute the Anaconda Plan.

Did you know?

- Cotton and slavery were so important to the Confederacy that cash printed by the Confederate government often depicted enslaved people working in cotton fields.

- Confederates avoided the term "civil war." They preferred "The War Between the States," believing that secession was permitted under the United States Constitution. The term remained popular among white southerners sympathetic to the Confederacy into the 20th century. They also labeled the struggle "The Second American Revolution" and "The War of Northern Aggression."

- Although only 11 states joined the Confederacy, the Confederate government recognized 13 states as members even though Kentucky and Missouri did not secede.

- The United States and Great Britain almost went to war over the construction of the Confederacy's commerce raiders, eventually forcing Great Britain to pay for the damage these raiders caused. The damages were collectively called the Alabama Claims, named for the Confederacy's most famous raider, the CSS Alabama.

- The first ironclad built by Confederate engineers was called the *CSS Virginia*, launched in early 1862. Reflecting the lack of industry in the South, the southerners built this ironclad from parts salvaged from a US Navy vessel called the *USS Merrimack*. US sailors scuttled that ship on the day Virginia seceded to prevent its capture.

- The *USS Monitor*, launched in early 1862, was an ironclad equipped with the first-ever rotating gun turret. The *USS*

Monitor and *CSS Virginia* confronted each other at the Battle of Hampton Roads in March 1862, the first battle in world history between ironclad warships.

SHILOH

Union General Ulysses S. Grant camped his Army of the Tennessee, numbering nearly 50,000 soldiers, in a thickly wooded and swampy area along the western bank of the Tennessee River in April 1862. His men needed rest. He also needed time for reinforcements to arrive. Grant's next move was southward, into Mississippi and toward the heavily fortified town of Vicksburg on the Mississippi River.

Grant had largely been a failure at the various jobs he'd tried during his life. Born in Ohio, he had settled in Illinois after attending West Point. He had been a mediocre student but a model officer during the Mexican-American War. He struggled as a farmer, bordering on bankruptcy. He tried tanning, turning animal skins into leather. Again, he struggled to make a living for himself and his family. The Civil War pulled Grant out of obscurity.

His lack of political connections or fame restricted him to what was called the Western Theater of the Civil War, the area between the Appalachian Mountains and the Mississippi River. Service in the Eastern Theater, the area between the Appalachian Mountains and the Atlantic Ocean, with fighting mostly focused on Virginia, would have to wait. The capitals at Richmond and Washington, D.C., in the Eastern Theater, were the prestigious positions within the armies of both sides.

Already, in early February 1862, Grant and his soldiers had captured the Confederate garrisons at Fort Henry, guarding the Tennessee River, and Fort Donelson, overlooking the Cumberland River. These major victories allowed Union ironclads to sail deep into central Tennessee. Grant also gained a nickname from his capture of Fort Donelson. Sending a note to the defending Confederate General, Grant wrote, "No terms except an unconditional and immediate surrender can be accepted." From that point, Ulysses S. Grant became "Unconditional Surrender" Grant.

With gunboats headed downriver to converge with another large Union Army approaching Nashville, Confederate generals retreated not only from the city but from most of central Tennessee. The Federals had captured the first capital of a Confederate state.

Grant now sat waiting for the army occupying Nashville to make its way to him. Once combined, Grant planned to launch the next leg of the campaign. Grant proved so confident - even overconfident - that he gave no attention to ordering his commanders to prepare defensive breastworks, walls behind which his troops could take positions in case of an attack. The victories of the last couple of months had led Grant to believe that the rebels had retreated far away to lick their wounds.

Confederate General Albert Sidney Johnston was far from licked. He gathered forces in northern Mississippi and plotted a surprise attack. He had to do something.

Southern politicians and editors raged against the quick fall of middle Tennessee with its capital. They howled for action that might push Grant's army back. Johnston, a lifelong officer in the US Army until his resignation in 1861, believed that an unexpected attack on Grant's troops might do more than push the Federals back. A surprise attack might even destroy Grant's entire army. Grant had, after all, made a major mistake. He had parked his army with its back to a wide river, making a quick retreat from a battle impossible.

Johnston's Confederate Army of nearly 45,000 men slammed into the unprepared Federal camps at dawn on April 6, 1862. Some Union soldiers were still asleep in their tents as musket fire broke the stillness.

The rebels were enthusiastic, despite the horrors of battle, as they realized they had the advantage. Confederate soldier Sam Watkins described the advance: "Men were lying in every conceivable position; the dead lying with their eyes wide open, the wounded begging piteously for help, and some waving their hats and shouting to us to go forward. It all seemed to me a dream."

The ferocious attack drove Grant's men toward the river. Valiant Federal soldiers tried desperately to hold back the rebel assault. The fighting was so heavy, though, that thousands of surprised Union soldiers fled the battlelines completely, scurrying to the river landing in the hope of escape. Grant, attempting to rally his men, recalled in his memoirs that "there probably were as many as four or five thousand stragglers lying under cover of the river bluff, panic-stricken, most of whom would have been shot where they lay, without resistance, before they would have taken muskets and marched to the front to protect themselves."

Two Federal gunboats, the *USS Tyler* and *USS Lexington*, provided covering fire for Grant's army.

A sunken road worn down by decades of wagon traffic near the center of the Federal line provided natural cover for a last-ditch effort to halt the rebels. The Yankees turned back several waves of attacks. In future accounts of the battle, this defensive line became celebrated as the Hornet's Nest.

The Confederates finally countered by concentrating 11 batteries with 53 cannons, one of the largest collections of artillery focused on firing at a single spot during the Civil War. Volley after volley blasted the defenders until over 2,000 Union soldiers and General Benjamin Prentiss, who had directed the defense of the Hornet's Nest, surrendered. Though captured, Prentiss's troops had bought precious time for Grant to stabilize his army.

Elsewhere on the battlefield, a bullet hit Gen. Johnston in the leg as he rode on horseback near the frontline during the mid-afternoon. He was urging on his exhausted Confederates. But the bullet had nicked a major artery. Within minutes, Johnston grew faint. In roughly an hour, Johnston lay dead. In the frantic chaos of combat, no one had thought to place a tourniquet on his leg to stop the bleeding. Albert Sidney Johnston was the highest-ranking general killed in battle during the Civil War.

The exhausted Confederates were unable to breach Grant's final defensive lines. The Union troops, knowing they had no further space to retreat, stayed firm. Night fell.

In the darkness, the long-awaited army from Nashville arrived, crossed the river, and reinforced the battered Union ranks with roughly 18,000 fresh troops. The Confederate commanders had expected to renew their attack the next day, finally capturing all that remained of Grant's men. Instead, the Federals counterattacked.

Another day of hard fighting left the Confederates on their heels. They slowly fell back across the blood-stained and body-strewn woods of the previous day's combat. When night finally descended on the second day, the rebel generals chose to withdraw their fatigued troops into Mississippi to regroup.

Looking back, Grant summarized the Battle of Shiloh: "It was a case of Southern dash against Northern pluck and endurance." His men had held.

In the South, the death of Johnston muted criticism of the failure to destroy Grant's army. Southern editors, like their northern counterparts, printed sheets listing the names of the killed and wounded to post outside their offices for worried families and friends to read. A teenage girl in New Orleans recorded in her diary the loud noise along the streets as newspaper offices printed the latest battle reports. Outside, she heard "such a slashing & crashing of windows, slamming of doors, whistlings & 'hurryings to and fro'" as neighbors rushed to grab a copy. When they finally read the news, the excitement turned to quiet. The Confederacy mourned.

Over 1,700 soldiers died on each side. Each side also suffered over 8,000 wounded. Thousands more were missing in action.

In the North, Grant received widespread criticism as the casualty reports arrived via northern newspapers. The death toll shocked everyone. Rumors circulated that Grant had been drunk. Others said Grant was incompetent.

Despite the pressure, President Lincoln refused to remove the General. Grant had achieved far more than Lincoln's more celebrated generals in the Eastern Theater or others in the Western Theater. About his decision to stick with Grant, Lincoln said, "I can't spare this man; he fights."

Did you know?

- Cavalry served as the "eyes and ears" of an army by scouting enemy positions. The thick woods and swamps at Shiloh reduced the effectiveness of cavalry, helping Johnston to surprise Grant.

- An army in the Civil War consisted of several corps organized into divisions. Divisions contained brigades formed of regiments. Regiments were divided into companies. Typically, regiments contained men from the same state.

- Soldiers at the start of the Civil War often elected their company officers.

- General Lew Wallace, a division commander serving under General Grant at Shiloh, wrote the novel *Ben-Hur* in 1880. The book ranked up with *Uncle Tom's Cabin* as the two best-selling novels of the 19th century.

- The famed novelist and humorist Mark Twain worked with General Grant to market his memoirs in the 1880s. The first printing of 350,000 quickly sold out.

- By the 1890s, the federal government preserved five Civil War battlefields as parks, the first effort to preserve any battlefields from the nation's various wars. These were Chattanooga-Chickamauga, Vicksburg, Shiloh, Antietam, and Gettysburg.

ANTIETAM

Confederate General Robert E. Lee launched a daring plan. The Army of the Potomac, under the command of Union General George McClellan, sat within sight of Richmond. McClellan had spent the summer of 1862 transporting his Union Army by boat to the east of the city before slogging up a swampy peninsula to get within firing range of the city. Lee now proposed a series of aggressive attacks to drive the Federals back toward the Atlantic Ocean before quickly turning northward into Maryland and Pennsylvania. With luck, the rebels could even cut some of the railroad lines leading to Washington, D.C., and lay siege to the United States capital.

A victory on northern soil might even convince a European power to recognize the Confederacy as an independent nation, providing an opportunity for foreign aid and assistance in breaking the Union blockade.

Lee, like McClellan, had served in the US Army during the Mexican-American War. Both had experience from years of military service. Lee's great strength was his ability as a strategist. He understood the complexity of moving large numbers of soldiers across wide areas. He also understood people, both in terms of finding good generals he could trust to carry out his strategy and in terms of recognizing the weaknesses of the Union generals who opposed his Confederate Army.

Lee knew McClellan was very cautious and slow to react. McClellan was an excellent organizer, but he was also a perfectionist. He refused to move until he felt he had ideal conditions. This hesitancy to act frustrated President Lincoln and caused McClellan to miss opportunities to strike the rebels at vulnerable moments.

Lee rose to command the Confederacy's largest army, the Army of Northern Virginia, in June 1862 after an artillery fragment wounded its previous commander. On taking charge of the army, he pressed forward, shocking McClellan with regular attacks. McClellan retreated.

With McClellan's battered army withdrawing and isolated on a peninsula in Virginia, Lee decided to turn to invade the North. The strategy aimed to accomplish several goals.

First, the unexpected campaign would take the war into Maryland and Pennsylvania. Such a move would force McClellan to pull the Union Army from Virginia to defend Washington, D.C. The deeper Lee advanced the rebels into the northern territory, the more McClellan would face public pressure to attack the

Confederates. If things played out as Lee hoped, he could carefully select the battlefield for this showdown, ensuring the best defensible position possible in order to inflict the most damage on his opponent.

Second, Lee planned to capture supplies stored at the Federal arsenal in Harpers Ferry, Virginia, protected by a small garrison of Union troops. The large stash of ammunition, muskets, uniforms, and other equipment promised to replenish the low supplies of the Confederates after having slugged it out with McClellan for most of summer 1862.

Third, Lee could also resupply his troops on land that had so far seen little fighting. Areas of northern Virginia were war-ravaged after a year of combat. Crops and animals were seized to feed the armies. Fences were torn down for firewood. But Maryland and Pennsylvania offered stocks of agricultural goods and herds of animals that could feed Lee's army, all while easing pressure on Virginia's farms. He also hoped to convince residents of the slave state to enlist, restocking the army with soldiers.

Fourth, Lee hoped to win a major battle deep within the United States. A victory in Maryland or, ideally, the free state of Pennsylvania, would demonstrate the strength of the Confederacy and the weakness of the United States. Such a win might convince Great Britain or France to recognize the Confederate States of America as an independent nation.

Neither European country, though eager for southern cotton, wanted to risk recognizing the Confederacy only to get dragged into a losing cause and a confrontation with the United States. But if Lee could win a battle in the North, then maybe the Confederacy could win the whole war. After all, Lee's primary military aim was to provoke the Union Army into attacking him, defeat that army on a battlefield that he could easily defend, and then, with Washington, D.C., left unguarded, march on the capital of the United States.

Lee's campaign started with shocking victories. His troops smashed a Union Army blocking his way near Bull Run Creek in late August 1862. Another rebel column then seized Harpers Ferry. By early September 1862, Lee had his army in Maryland moving northward.

Lee's remarkable success now faced a surprisingly active McClellan. Lincoln had ordered the Army of the Potomac back to Washington, D.C., to protect the capital. McClellan then received a lucky break. When Lee issued his plans for the campaign, one of his generals wrapped these orders outlining the Confederate Army's movements around three cigars. The general lost this package. A Union soldier found it and passed the enemy orders up the chain of command. McClellan suddenly knew where Lee's army was headed.

As McClellan's Army of the Potomac pursued the spread-out Army of Northern Virginia, Lee realized something was wrong. The Union forces were closing fast. He quickly identified an area around Sharpsburg, Maryland, to lay out his rebel units, issuing orders to meet along the hills overlooking Antietam Creek. The terrain made for a promising defensive position.

Lee's battleline was anchored north of Sharpsburg by thick woods with wheatfields in front. A small church on the edge of the woods, known as Dunker Church, provided more cover. The center of the Confederate line rested along a well-worn path called the Sunken Road. The road, known after the battle as Bloody Lane, provided the rebels with a natural trench to defend. The southern part of Lee's line focused on preventing Federal forces from crossing a stone bridge called, after the battle, Burnside Bridge for Union Gen. Ambrose Burnside, who received orders to cross it.

The Federals engaged the Confederates on September 17, 1862. McClellan arrived along Antietam Creek with 87,000 troops. Lee had barely 40,000 soldiers. Although he outnumbered the Army of Northern Virginia by two-to-one, McClellan refused to order an all-out attack. Instead, always cautious, the Union general hit different parts of the rebel line at different times. He punched Lee's left north of Sharpsburg in the morning. In the middle of the day, he struck Lee's center along the Sunken Road. In the afternoon, he hit Lee's right at Burnside Bridge. The piecemeal attacks allowed Lee to shift his men to reinforce vulnerable parts of his line.

By the late afternoon, it looked like the rebel army was on the verge of collapse. The afternoon attack had crossed Antietam Creek and was pushing toward Sharpsburg. Taking the town would have cut Lee's avenue of retreat. Luckily for Lee, reinforcements arrived from Harpers Ferry late in the day and slammed into the advancing Federals. The Union troops pulled back.

The battle shredded the ranks of Lee's Army of Northern Virginia. Over a quarter of the army had become casualties. Guts and luck had saved the rebels from disaster. But Lee did not retreat. He stayed put, daring McClellan to attack the next day. The cautious McClellan, shocked by the damage to his own army and convinced Lee had more troops, refused to test the thin lines of Confederate soldiers facing the Federals. Having rested his army for a day, Lee then chose to retreat back to Virginia.

McClellan remained still. Attacking Lee's excellent defensive line had mowed down the Union ranks. Almost 15% of the army had fallen as casualties. Some regiments had suffered a casualty rate of over 70%. That said, parts of the army, around 40% of

McClellan's troops, had not engaged Lee's forces and could have chased the rebels.

Frustrated, Lincoln met McClellan on the battlefield to urge him to take the offensive and crush Lee's army once and for all. The Union general still delayed as he resupplied and reinforced his battered units. A month later, Lincoln asked McClellan: "You remember my speaking to you of what I called your over-cautiousness. Are you not over-cautious when you assume that you cannot do what the enemy is constantly doing?" The next month, after McClellan still delayed, Lincoln removed McClellan from command.

Did you know?

- The Battle of Antietam is considered the bloodiest single day in US History. The Army of the Potomac registered 2,100 dead and 9,550 wounded. The Army of Northern Virginia listed 1,550 dead and 7,750 wounded.

- The arrival of Confederate reinforcements late in the battle confused the Federals because many of the rebel soldiers wore blue Federal uniforms captured from the arsenal at Harpers Ferry, Virginia.

- Future president William McKinley, in office from 1897 until 1901, served as a commissary officer responsible for feeding Union troops at the Battle of Antietam. In this role, McKinley delivered food and coffee to soldiers pinned down by heavy rebel fire for most of the day at Burnside Bridge.

- Union General Ambrose Burnside regularly shaved his face in a way that connected his mustache to his thick head of hair. His distinctive style became known as "Burnsides," a word that eventually changed to "sideburns."

- Alexander Gardner and his assistant James Gibson arrived two days after the Battle of Antietam to take photographs of the scene, becoming the first photographers to capture images of a Civil War battlefield. Their images of dead bodies shocked the American public.

- When Lincoln met McClellan several weeks after the battle, Alexander Gardner returned to Antietam to photograph the occasion. McClellan, standing 5 feet, 8 inches, arranged for Lincoln to sit in a chair so he'd look taller than the President. Lincoln refused. The famous photograph shows Lincoln, at 6 feet, 4 inches tall, towering over McClellan.

EMANCIPATION PROCLAMATION

Though Lincoln could not convince McClellan to turn the Battle of Antietam into a great military victory, the success of the Union Army in halting the Confederate invasion allowed Lincoln to use Antietam to achieve a great moral victory. He issued the Emancipation Proclamation in late September 1862, to take effect at the start of 1863.

Lincoln's document stated that in the new year "all persons held as slaves within any State or designated part of a State, the people whereof shall then be in rebellion against the United States, shall be then, thenceforward, and forever free; and the Executive Government of the United States, including the military and naval authority thereof, will recognize and maintain the freedom of such persons."

Lincoln acted because the enslaved within the Confederacy had complicated the Anaconda Plan. Everywhere the Federals marched or landed, they met enslaved African Americans fleeing plantations.

Life in enslavement was harsh. Some enslavers were harder on captive workers than others. But generally, African Americans received basic rations of corn, pork, and molasses along with a few clothes and a pair of shoes. Owners often encouraged African Americans to grow gardens to improve their diet without adding to costs. Enslavers pushed their workers to maximize farm profits.

Resistance to the whims of enslavers brought cruel punishments. Lucretia Alexander, an enslaved woman in Arkansas, recalled how owners abused the people they considered their property if those persons disobeyed or were caught after running away: "They put the dogs on him and they bit 'im and tore all his clothes off of 'im. Then they put 'im in the stocks. The stocks was a big piece of timber with hinges in it. It had a hole in it for your head." Once locked into the stocks, the enslaver "would lay that whip on you and you couldn't do nothin' but wiggle and holler."

The Civil War provided salvation from this life of hard work and torture in which families were regularly separated on the auction blocks of the South. The enslaved now gained their freedom with their feet, gathering around Union Army camps for protection.

Partly, these African Americans understood from conversations among their enslavers that Lincoln was anti-slavery. A few Union generals and officers were outspoken abolitionists. African Americans understood that the enemy of their enslavers had to be their ally. But the growing numbers of enslaved claiming their freedom presented President Lincoln with major legal and military problems as well as an opportunity to undermine the Confederacy.

Lincoln started the war championing the idea that the conflict was about preserving the Union, not ending enslavement. The President hoped to keep as many slave states as possible from joining the Confederacy, especially Kentucky and Maryland. To proclaim support for abolition risked pushing away these states. Lincoln also hoped to convince at least a few rebelling states to return to the United States.

After a year of fighting, the realization that the war might continue for years meant that Lincoln could not ignore the issue of enslavement any longer. However, he feared that declaring the emancipation of enslaved African Americans might look to white supremacist northerners like a desperate attempt to rescue a struggling war effort. This would hurt Lincoln politically in Congress. This would also hurt his ability to recruit troops from the predominantly white northern population.

News of McClellan's victory at Antietam gave Lincoln the cover to end the buying and selling of human beings, although only within the Confederacy. In other words, the Emancipation Proclamation ended enslavement but was enforceable only within the territory where Lincoln did not have authority.

This allowed Lincoln to free the enslaved who had already fled from within the Confederacy or who Union troops encountered as they pressed forward into rebel territory, draining the Confederates of manpower they used to grow crops or dig defenses. News of the Proclamation would also encourage thousands of more African Americans to flee the southern fields.

On the other hand, by permitting the trade in human beings to continue within Union lines as those stood on January 1, 1863, Lincoln ensured that the slave states within the United States remained loyal. He also guaranteed that arrangements in conquered areas were not disrupted. Lincoln even hoped that, by issuing the Proclamation in September 1862 with an effective date three months later, a state or two of the Confederacy might rejoin the Union in order to preserve slavery.

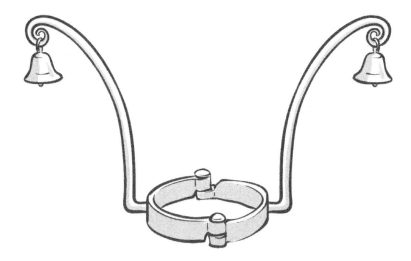

Lincoln played politics with the issue of enslavement. That said, he well understood the consequences of his action. The Proclamation recognized what was already being practiced by African Americans as they abandoned the plantations. Now Lincoln granted legal recognition of the freedom of millions of African Americans. During the final years of the war, Federal armies pushed deep into the Confederacy, guaranteeing their freedom.

Though slavery still existed within the United States, most people recognized that the Proclamation had set the country on the path to liberating all African Americans.

Importantly, the Proclamation changed the meaning and purpose of the war. Calls to restore the Union dominated talk in 1861 and 1862. From 1863 onward, the conflict became a war to end slavery. This made international recognition of the Confederacy harder to obtain for the rebels. European nations like Great Britain and France, both with large political movements urging more democracy, did not want to risk protests for backing a country fighting for slavery against another country proclaiming abolition.

With a stroke of a pen, Lincoln also fixed a manpower problem. Union commanders had hired the self-liberated enslaved who came to their lines. In return for supplies like food and clothing or even pay, these African Americans labored for themselves while assisting Federal soldiers. Women found work doing laundry and cooking. Men dug trenches or created breastworks to protect the Union troops.

These men, though, could not legally enlist. They were property in the United States that still recognized enslavement but did not recognize the Confederates as a separate country. This meant that the enslaved were still the Americans' property. Granting freedom to African Americans from the Confederacy allowed the Union Army to enlist these men, who were eager to liberate their friends and relatives still behind rebel lines.

Already in late 1862, African Americans in New Orleans, where a large population of nearly 10,000 lived as free people of color before the Civil War, volunteered as the 1st Louisiana Native Guards. In time, more units of the Louisiana Native Guard included the formerly enslaved. The fact that the

Louisiana Native Guard had black officers made the units unique in the Civil War.

Ordered into battle at Port Hudson, Louisiana, on the Mississippi River in 1863, the Louisiana Native Guard impressed everyone with their bravery. Captain Andre Cailloux, born into slavery, had worked hard to earn money doing odd jobs to pay for his freedom. A free man when the Civil War erupted, he helped mobilize the Louisiana Native Guard. He fell dead at Port Hudson, becoming a celebrated hero.

Despite the sacrifices of these units, the few units to have African American officers, most white Union soldiers refused to salute these men. White Union officers also often rejected African American officers as equals. Over time, these African American officers were removed in response to white supremacy within the Federal ranks.

Black soldiers commanded by white officers were common. The 54th Massachusetts Regiment is one of the most famed African American units with African American soldiers commanded by white officers. The unit gained national fame in a hard-fought assault at Fort Wagner on the South Carolina coast in July 1863.

Despite the courage shown by African American soldiers under fire, most black soldiers were restricted to duties away from the battlefront. These units of color guarded railroads and depots. African American soldiers dug trenches or worked the wagons driving supplies to the Union armies. Their job was hard labor. And they did so for less pay than that given to white soldiers of the same rank. Freedom from enslavement did not mean racial equality in the United States military during the Civil War.

Notwithstanding the discrimination these men faced, roughly 179,000 African Americans enlisted in the Union Army by the end of the war in 1865. This number represented 10% of the soldiers in the Federal ranks. An additional 19,000 manned ships were in the US Navy. Almost 40,000 of the African Americans in the armed services died.

These sacrifices helped win the freedom of millions of enslaved. But the future of these African Americans remained uncertain. Lewis Bonner, a formerly enslaved man born in Texas, recalled his wartime experiences in words that summarized the major change brought by the conflict and the major challenge faced by African Americans after emancipation. He explained, "I tell you it was some war. When it was all over, the Yankees came thoo' singing, 'You may die poor but you won't die a slave.'"

The question of poverty and access to economic opportunity for the freed people of color within the South remained for future Americans to confront. The buying and selling of human beings ended throughout the United States with the ratification of the Thirteenth Amendment in December 1865. But most African Americans across the South owned little other than themselves. They faced angry former enslavers hardened by years of war. They also confronted a belief in white supremacy that united white northerners with white southerners.

Opposing enslavement of human beings based on race was a major accomplishment of the United States during the Civil War. Supporting equality of all regardless of skin tone was a very different matter. This issue was only partially advanced by the Civil War.

Did you know?

- Before the Civil War, abolitionists operated a network of safe houses along routes enslaved people could use to escape the South. This network, known as the Underground Railroad, allowed roughly 100,000 African Americans between 1820 and 1860 to reach states banning slavery.

- Between 1830 and 1860, historians estimate over 30,000 African Americans fled to Canada, a colony of Great Britain. The Slavery Abolition Act in 1833 banned enslavement throughout Great Britain's empire. Many African Americans, whether born free or enslaved, feared for their safety so long as the United States accepted slavery as legal anywhere within its borders.

- The enslaved who fled to the Union Army before Lincoln issued the Emancipation Proclamation were called "contrabands" by US officials. "Contraband" is a word meaning "illegally transported goods." These human beings were considered enemy property.

- Harriet Tubman, arguably the most famous enslaved person to escape to the North along the Underground Railroad, worked tirelessly to liberate other enslaved people. During the Civil War, she volunteered to help the Union Army in South Carolina by scouting Confederate positions. She also encouraged hundreds of enslaved to flee to nearby Union camps.

- Captain P.B.S. Pinchback served as an officer in the 2nd Louisiana Native Guard. In 1872, he briefly rose to governor of Louisiana, the first African American to become a governor of any state in US History.

- During the 1930s, the United States government funded a program to interview, persons who had been born into enslavement. These interviews of their experiences are called the WPA Slave Narratives.

WOMEN AND
THE CIVIL WAR

One of the most popular songs performed on stage and in homes during the Civil War was "The Vacant Chair." The lyrics mourned the death of 18-year-old Union Lieutenant John William Grout on a battlefield in 1861: "At our fireside, sad and lonely, / Often will the bosom swell / At remembrance of the story / How our noble Willie fell."

Thousands of families who never knew Grout could relate to the description of his passing and the sadness felt by those who loved him because they too had lost relatives and friends in the war, if not more than one.

Though often far from the frontlines, women shaped the outcome of the Civil War as much as the men who enlisted. Maybe, at times, their influence was even stronger in the course of the conflict. Although not usually at the battlefront, women definitely experienced death and destruction as intensely as men.

Men and women during the early and mid-1800s lived in what historians call separate spheres. Men engaged with the world outside the home, known as the public sphere. They plowed and harvested fields. They took jobs or started businesses. They engaged in politics, both by voting and by campaigning for office.

The public sphere was a rough and tumble space of city streets and offices where violence frequently occurred. Men gambled; they smoked cigars and chewed tobacco; they drank large amounts of alcohol.

Some men rejected these vices, however, and participated with women in pushing for reforms to the public sphere. Organizations were created to ban alcohol, encourage healthy living, and boost church attendance, among other programs for improving American society.

Women engaged with the world inside the home, known as the private sphere. They raised children and ensured their education. They managed the household, cooking meals, cleaning the house, washing laundry, and hosting guests. Women also encouraged the family's religious devotion through saying prayers, reading from the Bible, and attending church.

Northern white families with money to spare hired domestic servants, often a young woman who had emigrated from

Ireland. Southern white families with spare wealth invested in an enslaved human being. In the Confederacy, just over 30% of white families owned an enslaved African American to aid with fieldwork or household chores.

When the Civil War erupted, white women on both sides encouraged men to enlist. Joining the fight meant protecting homes and families. This was the duty of men. Women shamed men who hesitated, suggesting that they lacked courage. A coward had no claim to manhood.

A few women were so enthusiastic about the war that they disguised themselves as men in order to enlist. Historians estimate that between 400 to 1,000 women served as soldiers, even seeing heavy combat. Some of these women enlisted to stay near a loved one. Some joined for the adventure. Others shared a sense of patriotism and duty.

Besides aiding in the recruitment of volunteers early in the war, women used the skills of the private sphere to equip the armies. Kate Stone, a girl on a Mississippi River plantation, scribbled a diary entry in May 1861: "Mamma has been busy all day sewing...shirts and going through the vegetable and flower garden." A few days later, Stone added, "We have been busy sewing today." She records in another entry: "Cakemaking, preserving, and peeling apples are the order of the day."

Preserving vegetables and fruits raised in the fields ensured a steady food supply. Sewing clothes kept households dressed. These duties grew more important with the outbreak of warfare. Part of the duties described by Stone meant sewing uniforms and flags for soldiers as well as providing them with food.

A few women left home to take jobs as nurses. They dressed wounds and encouraged soldiers with broken bodies to regain their strength. Their interaction with wounded soldiers provided the first step for men with wrecked bodies to recover a sense of their manhood.

The experiences of Cornelia Hancock, who traveled with the Army of the Potomac to care for the injured, give a glimpse into the stressful, bloody work nurses on both sides faced. She wrote home after a major battle in 1863: "To give you some idea of the extent and numbers of the wounds, four surgeons, none of whom were idle fifteen minutes at a time, were busy all-day amputating legs and arms. I gave every man that had a leg or arm off a gill of wine, to every wounded...one glass of lemonade, some bread and preserves."

Medical knowledge during the Civil War was more like butchering than salvaging bodies. This made the comforting presence of women - reminders of the private sphere associated with home - all the more important.

The wounded men who recovered, along with their grateful comrades in battered units, often wrote letters or gave gifts thanking nurses for their physical and emotional labor. One letter received by Cornelia Hancock from a soldier she nursed emphasized the calming reassurance she provided: "You little know the pleasure a Soldier feels in seeing a woman at camp."

As the war dragged into 1863 and beyond, women's encouragement of enlisted men wavered. Left at home to run households, women's duties expanded. Not only did they continue to manage their private sphere roles, but they also needed to assume tasks previously done by their fathers and husbands.

The expected months of warfare turned into years of absence. Death lists grew longer. The maimed bodies of veterans trickled home, but they were often too broken to return to their past careers. The chance of permanently losing a loved one dampened women's enthusiasm for the war effort.

Confederate women's support for the war wavered the most. Northern women could see some progress in the war, though slow in the first three years of the conflict. In the South, the Federal advance left farms stripped of goods and infrastructure damaged. Battlefields scarred more and more of the landscape. The value of Confederate money decreased in value as faith in victory wavered.

For enslaved African American women, the war brought hope but also worry. Union success promised freedom. But the hardships of war were felt as well. Enslaved women were more likely to remain with their enslavers than enslaved men.

Younger African American men attempted to escape to the Union lines most often. African American women were more wary of the risks. The possibility of recapture and punishment was a fear that kept many African American women, especially those with children to protect, with their enslavers.

The tightening of the Union blockade slowly reduced stockpiles of medicines, fabrics, and other items from Europe, making life harder for all southern women. The disruption of trade with the United States also cut off rebel homes from goods raised on northern farms and produced in northern factories.

By 1863, the high cost of wheat, a crop largely raised in the midwestern United States, made bread scarce in the Confederacy. Women in Richmond, Savannah, and other southern cities launched occasional riots, smashing grocery stores and other stores to steal the food they needed for their families.

The departure of fighting-aged white men encouraged enslaved African Americans to grow rebellious against the authority of their enslavers, even if these African Americans were still too afraid to risk the consequences of fleeing and leaving enslaved family members behind. They increasingly disobeyed instructions and voiced criticism of their enslavers. This rebelliousness left white women afraid.

Increasingly, southern white women wrote letters to their husbands, fathers, brothers, and sons away in the army describing the worsening conditions back home. This demoralized many soldiers within the rebel ranks. Some women outright asked these men to come home.

Desertion rates among Confederate units were as high as 15%, compared to a high of 12% among Union units. With a much smaller population to draw upon, the higher desertion rate greatly worried Confederate officials. The problem worsened as defeat seemed more and more likely in 1864 and 1865.

By 1864, some areas of the Confederacy openly opposed government officials, especially when military units arrived to catch deserters or confiscate crops and livestock for use by the rebel army.

Resistance grew so intense in Jones County, Mississippi, that it became known as the Free State of Jones. A legend arose that the community seceded from Mississippi and the Confederacy.

The morale of women, along the home front, heavily influenced the morale of the men on the battlefront. Ultimately, southern white women's support of the war faltered the most as Confederate armies failed to push back the Federals and Confederate politicians could not figure out a way to lift the tightening Union blockade.

But even into late 1864, most women on both sides held to a stubborn belief that victory would come. Before the war ended, however, the conflict became much deadlier for both sides and, for the Confederates, much more devastating.

Did you know?

- The Seneca Falls Convention held in New York in 1848 was the first women's rights gathering in the United States. The Convention launched the effort to give women the right to vote, a right finally won with the ratification of the Nineteenth Amendment in 1920.

- After shooting a Union soldier who entered her home, Isabella "Belle" Boyd of Virginia, a teenager, became an infamous Confederate spy. As a young woman, she was not at first suspected of espionage. She easily rode past Union guards to relay information about Federal movements. Boyd was eventually arrested six times and imprisoned three times.

- Born in Massachusetts in 1821, Clara Barton served as a Union nurse during the Civil War. She earned the nickname "Angel of the Battlefield." She continued her humanitarian efforts after the war, establishing the American Red Cross in 1881. She remained president of the organization until her retirement in 1904.

- Louisa May Alcott, born in Pennsylvania in 1832, worked as a Union nurse. She used this experience to write her first book, *Hospital Sketches*, in 1863. Alcott gained national recognition as an author with the bestselling novel *Little Women* published in 1868.

- Born in 1832, Mary Edwards Walker of New York studied medicine at a time when only men were allowed to become doctors. She famously broke gender norms by being one of the first women to wear pants. During the

Civil War, Walker became the first woman to serve as a U.S. Army surgeon and the first woman to receive the Congressional Medal of Honor.

- After the Civil War, white women of the former Confederacy celebrated the manhood of the region's defeated, and often severely wounded, white men by raising money to erect hundreds of statues of Confederate leaders and common soldiers. This effort was led by the United Daughters of the Confederacy.

GETTYSBURG

After Antietam and the removal of General McClellan, Lincoln promoted several generals, each with disastrous results. Again and again, Confederate General Robert E. Lee inflicted embarrassing defeats.

Union General Ambrose Burnside attacked a heavily fortified position at Fredericksburg, Virginia, in December 1862. With the rebels behind a stone wall and supporting artillery on the hill above the infantry, the Confederates ripped gaping holes in the attacking Federals.

Lincoln then replaced Burnside with General Joseph Hooker. In a daring move, Lee split his Confederate Army despite being outnumbered nearly two-to-one. He sent an attack wing to hit the Union Army from an unexpected direction while the other wing kept Hooker's focus. The charging rebels stunned the Federals, overrunning encampments and forcing Hooker to withdraw with heavy casualties. Hooker's defeat in the Battle of Chancellorsville in late May 1863 convinced Lincoln to make another change in command.

Lincoln now appointed General George Meade to head the Army of the Potomac. Meade had his work cut out for him. He had to repair the damaged Union Army and chase down Lee's troops, who were on the offensive.

As in the previous year, Lee recognized an opportunity to seize the initiative while the Union Army reeled from the loss at Chancellorsville. His Army of Northern Virginia numbered roughly 75,000 strong. A couple of hundred cannons added to their firepower. The troops were confident after their impressive victory over Hooker's troops. With the war entering its third year, Lee knew he had no time to waste given the worsening shortages of manpower and supplies.

Lee gathered his forces and moved northward. He launched another campaign aiming for Maryland and Pennsylvania in an effort to draw Union units out of Virginia, where the civilian population had borne the brunt of the fighting. Again, he hoped to force a major battle on northern soil that might win foreign recognition for the Confederacy and leave Washington, D.C., vulnerable to capture.

The push into Pennsylvania went smoothly. Lee's men seized supplies in areas where no army had marched. A column of his army moved to Gettysburg because rumors suggested a stockpile of shoes and boots could be found in the town. As the rebel infantry approached the outskirts on July 1, 1863, a line of Union cavalry confronted them.

The sound of gunfire attracted the attention of the armies on both sides. Lee's generals and Meade's generals started rushing troops to the scene. Confederate generals thought the Federal cavalrymen were a small force easily brushed aside. They didn't realize Meade had rushed the Army of the Potomac to intercept Lee's columns. Unexpectedly for Lee and Meade, their armies had now met and engaged.

From the evening of the first day of fighting and into the next morning, Meade positioned over 100,000 soldiers and more than 300 cannons south of Gettysburg along a line shaped like an upside-down, backward "J." The northern part of the line was anchored by a wooded, hilly area known as Culp's Hill. The center ran along high ground called Cemetery Ridge.

Lee opened the second day of fighting by testing Meade's line at both ends. The Confederates attacked Culp's Hill while another attack charged the left edge of Meade's defenses along Cemetery Ridge. The Union commander rushed 20,000 troops to this end of his line, realizing that a hill called Little Round Top was key to the battlefield.

If the Confederates took Little Round Top, the rebels could rain artillery shells upon the Union line from behind, collapsing the Federals' position. The fighting for Little Round Top and a rocky area at the base of the hill called Devil's Den was some of the fiercest of the battle. Meade's men held despite intense pressure from the Confederates. The Federals dug in around Little Round Top.

Convinced his attacks had drawn most of Meade's forces to the right and left edges of the Union line, Lee planned a massive assault against Meade's center on the third day of battle.

Some Confederate generals disagreed with their commander. They believed the best course was to renew attacks at the fringes of Meade's defenses in an attempt to reach behind the Army of the Potomac, forcing a collapse. They also argued that an attack on the center was suicidal. Confederate soldiers would need to cross nearly a mile of open fields, leaving them vulnerable to artillery fire throughout the advance and heavy musket fire in the last few hundred yards of the charge. Lee held firm.

Lee ordered 12,000 soldiers to attack Meade's center. General George Pickett's units took the lead. Following a strong artillery barrage to weaken the Union troops stationed there, Confederate infantry rushed across the field. Despite taking heavy casualties, the rebels broke the Union line. But counterattacks drove the rebels back, closing the gap. The attack, which became known as Pickett's Charge, had failed. Half the men in the assault became casualties.

The armies of Lee and Meade stared at each other on July 4. Lee hoped Meade might attack, giving the Confederates the advantage of fighting from defensive positions. Meade did not take the bait. In the afternoon, Lee ordered a retreat back to Virginia.

The biggest, deadliest battle of the Civil War was over. Meade reported over 3,100 dead and 14,500 wounded. Another 5,300 were missing or captured. Lee recorded over 3,900 killed and 18,700 wounded. An additional 5,400 were missing or captured. Roughly 25% of the Army of the Potomac and close to 40% of the Army of Northern Virginia had been lost.

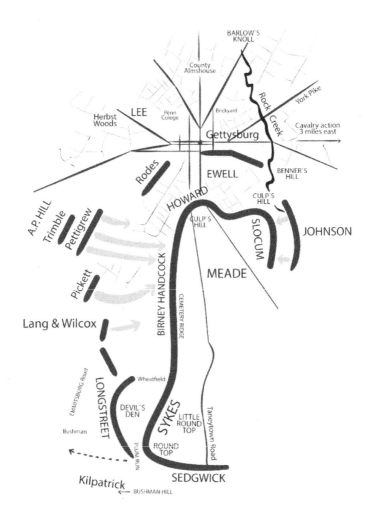

Meade had won a great victory. But the damage to the Army of the Potomac shocked the country. Meade stayed put to resupply and regroup rather than direct his battered army toward Lee's withdrawing rebels.

But several regiments of Meade's army, consisting of 4,000 troops, had no time to rest. They were rushed to New York City where rioters in mid-July 1863 were protesting the draft, a process that forced eligible men into the army. Poor whites, many of them Irish immigrants, expressed anger at being forced to enlist in an army fighting for the liberation of enslaved African Americans. These resisters attacked African American neighborhoods. During several days of attacks, over a hundred people died.

President Lincoln appreciated the significance of Gettysburg and the draft riot. He decided to travel to the battlefield for the opening of the cemetery where the thousands of dead would be buried. It proved an opportunity for Lincoln to redefine the war's aims, justifying commitment to the struggle as a war for freedom for all.

Lincoln's Gettysburg Address was a solemn, brief statement now considered one of the most powerful political speeches ever given by a president. He spent weeks crafting the words. On November 19, 1863, Lincoln delivered a speech to a large crowd. He began, "Four score and seven years ago our fathers brought forth on this continent a new nation, conceived in liberty, and dedicated to the proposition that all men are created equal."

Lincoln mourned the dead. He also called on Americans to remain dedicated to achieving victory. He closed, "It is rather for us to be here dedicated to the great task remaining before us, that from these honored dead we take increased devotion to that cause for which they gave the last full measure of devotion, that we here highly resolve that these dead shall not have died in vain, that this nation, under God, shall have a new birth of freedom, and that government of the people, by the people, for the people, shall not perish from the earth."

Did you know?

- The Army of Northern Virginia reached its peak in manpower in the summer of 1862, when it contained around 92,000 troops. Casualties slowly shrank the army over the next three years of combat because the Confederacy had a much smaller population than that of the northern United States.

- Over 3,000 horses died during the Battle of Gettysburg. Horses were essential to 19th-century armies for moving wagons and artillery. Generals and other high-ranking officers also rode on horseback to deliver orders quickly and to observe the terrain.

- Historians believe that the well-read Lincoln modeled his Gettysburg Address on a speech known as the Funeral Oration by Pericles in 430 BCE. Pericles, a political leader in the ancient Greek city-state of Athens, led the Athenians during the Peloponnesian War, a conflict waged among the various Greek cities.

- Lincoln's Gettysburg Address lasted only two minutes. Other speakers at the cemetery dedication spoke for an hour or longer, common for speeches in the 19th century. Lincoln's speech was so unexpectedly short that photographers were unable to capture the President speaking. Three photographs exist of Lincoln after the speech.

- As late as 1996, remains of the dead from the battle were still being discovered in the fields around Gettysburg. A year later, the body was buried with full military honors in Gettysburg National Military Park Cemetery.

- In 2023, an archeologist digging near Little Round Top discovered an unexploded artillery shell from the battle. A bomb disposal unit from the US Army removed the deadly ordnance.

VICKSBURG

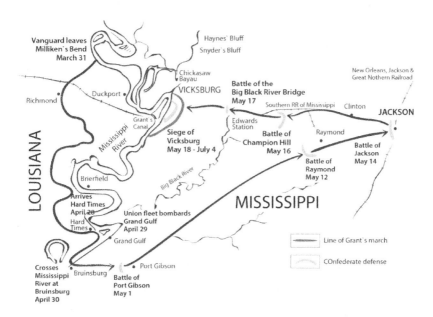

The Union victory at Gettysburg was not the only cause for celebration across the United States.

As Lee's army retreated from the hills of Pennsylvania, news of an equally important victory deep in the Confederacy at Vicksburg, Mississippi, sent electric currents through the telegraph wires, the quickest way to send messages in the 19th century. General Grant's Union Army had captured the strongest fortress on the Mississippi River.

After surviving Shiloh, Grant returned his focus to pushing along the Mississippi River to remove the Confederate forts. He aimed to liberate the waterway for military and commercial use, in accord with the Anaconda Plan.

President Lincoln was particularly eager to free the river for trade. Some of his most staunch political critics were in the Midwest, states like Ohio and Indiana, among others. Farmers here normally sent their crops downriver to New Orleans, as Lincoln knew from his days operating a flatboat. Lincoln also needed the river to resupply the US Navy on blockade duty in the Gulf of Mexico more rapidly.

Situated high on bluffs overlooking the river, Vicksburg was a formidable obstacle. Grant's first thought as he approached from the north in late spring 1863 was to dig a large ditch that might change the course of the Mississippi River. He did not want to risk the lives of his 75,000 troops in an assault. The attempt failed.

Determined to take the city, Grant then launched one of the most daring military campaigns in history. He marched his army down the swampy western bank of the river well away from Vicksburg's guns. He then crossed his men to the eastern bank roughly 30 miles downriver from the city. A fleet of gunboats ran past the cannons bristling from Vicksburg to help ferry Grant across the water. But rather than advance on Vicksburg, Grant's army headed to Jackson, the capital of the state, before turning back toward his main target.

The risks were enormous. Grant's force moved through hostile territory largely separated from his supply base on the river. His plan called for the Union Army to seize goods from farms along the way, giving it greater independence of movement without much concern for attacks on his supply line. Grant thus solved two issues - resupplying his army and depleting supplies available to the rebels.

The movements of Grant's forces surprised Confederate General John Pemberton, who commanded the 33,000 soldiers at

Vicksburg. He feared weakening his garrison at Vicksburg by going after Grant, believing the Union advance inland might be a decoy. By the time he realized his error, it was too late. Grant had captured Jackson.

But rather than stay put, Grant seized supplies at Jackson, destroyed the railroad, and burned anything that might aid the Confederate Army before turning toward Vicksburg.

As the Union forces under Grant's command approached the fortress city, General Pemberton sent columns of Confederate soldiers to block the path. He also pleaded with the Confederate government for reinforcements. But rebel leaders could not spare troops from elsewhere to rescue the southern soldiers now trapped inside Vicksburg.

Intense fighting occurred between Jackson and Vicksburg, a distance of about 50 miles. George Washington Cable, a teenager in the Confederate ranks, recalled the confusion as the rebel army folded under heavy fire at the Battle of Champions Hill. Artillery units worked desperately to turn the tide.

Cable described how the rebel cannon crews "trotted round and unlimbered and the Federal guns vomited their fire point-blank and blue skirmishers crackled and the gray line crackled back, and while lead and iron whined and whistled, and chips, sand and splinters flew, and a dozen boys dropped," the batteries loaded, fired, and reloaded again. The officers in charge "gave directions to each piece by number, for 'solid shot,' or 'case' or 'double canister.'" But all was lost. The rebels retreated to Vicksburg's trenches.

Grant followed closely, surrounding the city to the east with his army and to the west with Federal ironclads. Grant assaulted the heavily entrenched Confederates. The high casualties from these failed attacks convinced Grant to stop his offensive. Instead, he'd wait. Time was on his side.

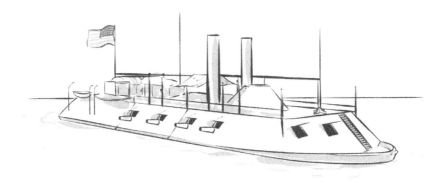

Grant had decided to lay Vicksburg under siege. With the 50 miles behind his army stripped bare during the march from Jackson, he had little worry about a Confederate relief army sneaking up from behind. The Union Army brought in artillery to shell the rebels.

Occasionally, Grant ordered assaults to probe the Confederate trenches to test for weaknesses. Once, he had miners dig a tunnel from the Union trenches to beneath the Confederate defenses. They planted explosives. The detonation was coordinated with a massive assault that Grant hoped would break the rebel lines. It failed.

The siege lasted 47 days. The rebels ran low on supplies. Desperately hungry, the Confederate soldiers, along with 4,600 civilians living in Vicksburg, ate rats and dogs. Some civilians escaped the constant shelling by Union artillery by digging deep caves into the bluffs near the Mississippi River.

Finally, on July 4, 1863, General Pemberton surrendered to General Grant. Vicksburg had been taken. Within a few weeks, the last fort on the Mississippi River, at Port Hudson, Louisiana, fell too. The United States had reclaimed the Mississippi River.

The southern men who survived the siege were paroled upon their capture. In the honor-driven society of the 19th century United States, a man's word was his bond. On the promise not to take up arms until notified by his government, a prisoner-of-war could return home. Only after an official exchange of prisoners occurred - on paper between officials in Washington, D.C., and Richmond - could a captured soldier be allowed back into the army.

The parole system was convenient for warring governments. Holding a prisoner meant spending resources on them, such as clothing and food. It also meant imprisoning them under guard.

On the other hand, a soldier captured by the enemy went safely home. Men could return to their families. They could farm. They couldn't return to the battlefront until exchanged, but they stabilized the home front.

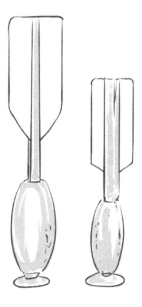

Under this system, Grant paroled the 30,000 rebels captured at Vicksburg. But within months, these men reappeared in the Confederate armies without being exchanged. The rebel commanders were too short on manpower to respect the exchange system. Soon, the governments of the United States and the Confederate States refused to parole any prisoners.

The Confederate Congress at the request of President Jefferson Davis issued an order regarding prisoners a couple of months before Vicksburg's fall that had already soured relations between the United States and the Confederate States regarding paroles. Davis aimed to stop the Federals' enlistment of African Americans officially freed by President Lincoln's Emancipation Proclamation and their use in battles against their former enslavers. He also took aim at the white officers leading these soldiers of color.

The Confederate Congress authorized President Davis "to cause full and ample retaliation" for President Lincoln's attempt to undermine enslavement. A white officer leading African American soldiers, if captured, "shall be deemed as inciting servile insurrection, and shall, if captured, be put to death, or be otherwise punished at the discretion of the [military] court."

African American soldiers if taken prisoner were to "be delivered to the authorities of the State or States in which they shall be captured, to be dealt with according to the present or future laws of such State or States." State laws across the Confederacy authorized the death penalty for an enslaved person involved in a slave insurrection.

President Lincoln threatened to execute Confederate prisoners-of-war for every African American soldier or white officer executed if President Davis acted on these resolutions by the Confederate Congress. Davis did not challenge Lincoln.

Instead, the parole and exchange system froze. If rebels captured African Americans, they were typically put to work or, when possible, returned to their enslaver.

For both sides, prisoners taken from mid-1863 onward increasingly landed in a stockade.

In the North, captured rebels were placed in large outdoor facilities enclosed by large walls, as at Elmira Prison in New York or Camp Douglas in Illinois. One rebel holding area was Johnson Island in Ohio sitting in Lake Erie. Another was in a Maryland peninsula sticking into the Chesapeake Bay. These windswept areas chilled the prisoners. As the war dragged on, these stockades became overcrowded. Death rates were high.

In the South, captured Federals were also placed in outdoor facilities. Lacking the resources of the North, however, these prisoners of war suffered severely. Food and supplies were meager. The Confederates already had difficulty feeding themselves much less thousands of captured Yankees. The most notorious Confederate prison opened at Andersonville, Georgia, in 1864. Built to hold 8,000 men, the camp reached a peak of 32,000 prisoners. Of the 45,000 total men held there during the existence of the stockade, nearly 13,000 died from disease, starvation, and execution.

Captain Henry Wirz, the Confederate superintendent of the stockade at Andersonville, was tried, convicted, and executed for war crimes, one of two rebels who was tried and punished after the Civil War. The other man was a Confederate guerilla named Champ Ferguson who was active in the states of Kentucky, Tennessee, and Virginia. The charges against Ferguson included his execution of wounded and captured African American cavalrymen and their white officers.

Did you know?

- Confederate General John C. Pemberton was from Philadelphia, Pennsylvania. Two of his brothers fought for the Union. Pemberton joined the Confederacy at the urging of his wife, born in Virginia. Pemberton gave up Vicksburg on July 4 because he believed his soldiers might receive more sympathy by surrendering on the United States' Independence Day.

- William Ketchum, an inventor and former mayor of Buffalo, New York, recognized that the Union Army would be fighting rebels in defensive positions. He designed one of the world's earliest hand grenades in 1861. Named the Ketchum Hand Grenade, the device looked like a large dart. These were used at Vicksburg and other sieges.

- Most residents of Vicksburg refused to celebrate Independence Day after the city fell to General Grant. The holiday passed quietly until July 4, 1947, when General Dwight Eisenhower, the supreme Allied commander in Europe during the Second World War and future president, visited the city. Ever since Vicksburg has honored the nation's birthday.

- In the 1960s, archeologists discovered the resting place of the *USS Cairo*, an ironclad sunk by a mine on the Yazoo River north of Vicksburg. The vessel was raised from the river bottom and remains on display at Vicksburg National Military Park, a rare surviving example of the wartime river navy.

- Prisoner stockades in the Civil War often had a marked-off line inside near the outer walls. Captives were automatically shot if they crossed. The line was called the "deadline," a word that then became common in American English for due dates.

- Dedicated in 2004, the governments of Mississippi and Vicksburg paid $250,000 to erect a monument commemorating the service of African American soldiers and civilians during the Vicksburg campaign. This monument, out of 1,300 monuments in Vicksburg National Military Park, is the only one dedicated to African Americans and one of the few on any preserved Civil War battlefield.

THE OVERLAND CAMPAIGN

President Lincoln promoted General Grant to overall command of the Western Theater shortly after the capture of Vicksburg. Grant's first task was to rescue a trapped Union Army in Chattanooga, Tennessee. Grant's success led Lincoln to award another promotion. He had found a general who knew how to win everywhere he marched.

In March 1864, Lincoln made Grant a Lieutenant General. No one had held that rank since George Washington.

General Grant now went to Virginia to coordinate a fresh Union campaign to crush the Confederacy. But while previous generals had fixated on capturing Richmond, Grant understood the rebel capital to be the means to an end. He planned to destroy General Lee's Army of Northern Virginia.

General Grant had learned valuable lessons from fighting in the Western Theater. At Shiloh, he learned the importance of never losing sight of his enemy. At Vicksburg, he learned his army could largely live off supplies gained from enemy farms. He also realized that he could pin down the rebels if he targeted the right spot. Vicksburg had been too important for the Confederates to abandon.

Early in the war, the rebels likely could have surrendered Richmond without destroying white southerners' will to fight. The idea of independence was more important than a national capital that had already moved from Alabama to Virginia. But by 1864, too much blood had been shed defending Richmond. The city had become symbolic of Confederates' resistance. The fall of Richmond would announce that independence was a lost cause.

Grant knew Lee would have to defend Richmond. Grant also knew he had more men and more supplies.

Directing the Union armies, he ordered General Meade's Army of the Potomac to march toward the Confederate capital in May 1864. He also commanded another Union Army to move down the nearby Shenandoah Valley, an agricultural region of Virginia known as the Confederacy's breadbasket for the large quantities of wheat raised there. Grant wanted to maximize pressure on the rebels by striking hard from various directions at the same time, stretching the Confederates' already thin ranks.

General Lee positioned his Army of Northern Virginia, numbering around 66,000 men, in a heavily wooded area north of Richmond to block the Union Army. The Army of the Potomac, with over 115,000 soldiers, slammed into the rebels, taking heavy casualties at the Battle of the Wilderness. Despite suffering nearly double the losses inflicted on Lee's army, Grant refused to retreat.

Instead, Grant maneuvered the Union Army past Lee's men to slip closer to Richmond. Lee again took defensive positions to block the advance. At the Battle of Spotsylvania Court House, the Union Army repeated its attack on Lee. And again, it suffered heavy losses - 2,725 killed, another 13,416 wounded, and 2,258 missing or captured. Lee's army had 1,515 killed, another 5,414 wounded, and 5,758 missing or captured.

Facing intense criticism for the high cost of lives, Grant refused to withdraw as previous Union commanders like McClellan, Burnside, and Hooker had done. Grant declared of the bloodshed, "I propose to fight it out on this line if it takes all summer."

It took much longer than the summer of 1864. The Army of Potomac slid further southward toward Richmond, forcing the battered Army of Northern Virginia to follow. By the end of May, Grant's forces were within striking distance of the Confederate capital.

At the Battle of Cold Harbor in early June 1864, Grant ordered a frontal assault on Richmond's outer fortifications to test for weaknesses. The attack was disastrous. The Army of the Potomac suffered over 12,700 casualties compared to the rebels' nearly 5,200 casualties.

Grant refused to ease the pressure. But he realized that frontal assaults were too costly. The solution was to dig trenches in front of Richmond and slowly stretch those trenches southward toward the neighboring town of Petersburg, a key railroad crossroads vital to supplying the Confederate capital. The strategy forced the Confederates to stretch their trench lines as well to counter the Yankees. Like stretching a rubber band, Grant planned to force Lee to extend the Army of Northern Virginia until it was so thin that it broke.

The Civil War in Virginia now became a brutal conflict of trench warfare. For the next ten months until early April 1865, the primary Union and Confederate armies were in a death grip. Grant, outnumbering his enemy by two-to-one, planned to bleed Lee's army dry.

The other part of Grant's plan, a move by another Union army down the Shenandoah Valley in May 1864 to coincide with the advance of the Army of the Potomac, made equally impressive headway - though the army stalled over the summer.

General Lee, desperate to turn back the Union army in the Shenandoah Valley and draw troops out of the Union army around Richmond, ordered a small Confederate army to advance toward Washington, D.C. This rebel force even pushed into Pennsylvania, burning the town of Chambersburg. But as Union troops converged on them, the Confederates retreated to Virginia.

Frustrated with this gutsy invasion of Pennsylvania by the enemy, Grant ordered a trusted and aggressive General Philip Sheridan to reorganize the Union units in the Shenandoah Valley and drive the rebels out once and for all.

Grant wanted no more surprise offensives by the rebels. He told Sheridan: "Do all the damage to railroads and crops you can." He explained, "If the war is to last another year, we want the Shenandoah Valley to remain a barren waste."

Sheridan launched his campaign in August 1864. He hit hard the Confederate forces he encountered. He ordered his army to strip the Valley of anything that could be used by the rebels. When he finished his push through the Valley by mid-October 1864, he wrote Grant, "I have destroyed over 2,000 barns filled with wheat, hay and farming implements; over 70 mills, filled with flour and wheat; have driven in front of the army over 4,000 head of stock, and have killed and issued to the troops not less than 3,000 sheep."

The Shenandoah Valley had been stripped bare and torched.

Finished with the campaign, the bulk of Sheridan's army joined the trenches around Richmond to apply more pressure on the rebel defenses.

The final showdown between the two largest armies of the United States and the Confederate States was now a test of wills over who could outlast the other.

Did you know?

- As volunteers became sparse, the Confederacy, in April 1862, introduced a military draft of all white men between 18 and 35 years old for three years. In September 1862, the government increased the age to 45. In February 1864, the draft required all white men between 17 and 50 to serve until the end of the war.

- The Confederate draft was highly controversial and unpopular with poor white southerners. The government allowed the wealthy to pay a substitute otherwise exempt from the draft to serve in his place. The law also exempted one white man for every 20 enslaved persons owned. Poor white southerners increasingly criticized the war as a "rich man's war and a poor man's fight."

- With more manpower than the Confederacy, the United States did not institute a draft until March 1863, the first in the nation's history. All men between 20 and 45 years old could be drafted. A draftee could pay a substitute to serve instead or pay $300 to the government for an exemption.

- As at Vicksburg, General Grant ordered miners to dig beneath a vulnerable spot along the Confederate trenches around Richmond. The resulting Battle of the Crater on July 30, 1864, ended in disaster. Union attackers charged into, instead of around, the crater created by the explosion. The Union absorbed 3,700 casualties to the Confederates' nearly 1,500 casualties.

- The shocking number of dead and wounded from General Grant's attacks in the battles of the Wilderness,

Spotsylvania, and Cold Harbor led some northern newspapers to condemn the general's strategy. Editors gave him a new nickname: "Butcher."

- During the Civil War, one in seven soldiers listed as wounded eventually died from their wounds. Civil War medicine was very primitive with limited knowledge about preventing bacteria from causing infections.

THE MARCH TO THE SEA

General Grant's strategy of latching the Army of the Potomac tightly to General Lee's Army of Northern Virginia near Richmond and devastating the Shenandoah Valley formed part of a much wider plan to apply pressure everywhere possible. This prevented reinforcements from reaching Lee while depleting the Confederacy's manpower and supplies.

Grant promoted General William Tecumseh Sherman to command the Union's western armies. Sherman was tasked with carrying out Grant's strategy in Georgia, in the middle of the Confederacy.

Born in Ohio in 1820, Sherman served in the military during the Mexican-American War before briefly becoming a banker. His brothers entered law and politics. On the eve of the Civil War, Sherman became a school superintendent in Louisiana. When war erupted, he commanded a brigade at First Bull Run before serving under Grant at Shiloh and Vicksburg.

Now in command of the Western Theater, Sherman planned to lead the Army of the Ohio, Army of the Tennessee, and Army of the Cumberland - totaling over 110,000 soldiers - on a campaign against the Confederate Army of Tennessee, numbering nearly 54,000 troops, commanded by General Joseph Johnston.

Sherman ordered the advance in May 1864 at the same time that Grant launched the Overland Campaign against Richmond, Virginia.

Sherman directed his army against Atlanta, a vital railroad crossroads that the Confederates had to defend. He maneuvered his men southward from Tennessee through the mountainous terrain of northern Georgia. Johnston's rebels guarded the passes, attempting to provoke Sherman into costly assaults. Instead, Sherman ordered his men to flank the Confederates, meaning to move around the end of the rebels' entrenchments.

Sherman used his larger army to stretch Johnston's defensive line until the Confederate commander had to retreat to prevent the Federals from encircling the southerners. At defensive line after defensive line, the Confederates were forced to withdraw, even after Johnston received reinforcements of 15,000 men. The extra troops briefly made Johnston's army the biggest in the Confederacy.

The warfare waged by Grant and Sherman no longer involved lines of men facing each other and blasting away, as in the early years of the war. The modern age of the rifled musket and rifled cannon had too much range and accuracy to use tactics learned from prior wars, before the rifling of firearms and artillery.

Seasoned veterans survived by taking cover. Ambrose Bierce, an officer serving in Sherman's army who survived a glancing bullet blow to his head, recalled the inglorious shift in tactics practiced during the Atlanta campaign and elsewhere during the last years of the war. Bierce wrote, "When battles are going on in open ground it frequently occurs that the opposing lines, confronting each other within a stone's throw for hours, hug the earth as closely as if they loved it."

Even commanders opted to survive rather than unnecessarily risk being hit. Bierce continued, "The line officers in their proper places flatten themselves no less, and the field officers, their horses all killed or sent to the rear, couch beneath the infernal canopy of hissing lead and screaming iron without a thought of personal dignity."

Frustrated at the failure of Johnston to halt Sherman's armies, Confederate President Jefferson Davis replaced him with a more reckless commander. The attacks launched by the new commander decimated his southern troops.

Soon, Sherman had Atlanta largely encircled. The surviving Confederates had to retreat or be captured. Atlanta fell into Union hands on September 2, 1864.

The capture of Atlanta rescued President Lincoln, who was facing an election. Lincoln was running as a candidate for the National Union Party, selecting a Democrat named Andrew Johnson of Tennessee as his vice-president. Lincoln, by abandoning the Republican Party label, looked to make the election a referendum on finishing the Civil War, uniting Republicans with pro-war Democrats.

Lincoln faced stiff competition in the election from the Democratic candidate, former General George McClellan. The Union general relieved by Lincoln years earlier now advocated signing a peace deal with the rebels.

The Democratic Party contained some of the sharpest critics of Lincoln from the time of his election. Democrats' complaints about the President's leadership sometimes extended to open support for the Confederacy. Supporters of the President and his efforts to restore the Union raised accusations of treason against these Democrats. Democrats who outrightly opposed the war, demanding an immediate peace agreement, were denounced as disloyal "Copperheads," a poisonous snake common within the eastern United States.

With Grant and Sherman taking heavy casualties through the summer of 1864 without much progress, McClellan seriously challenged Lincoln's hope to get reelected and finish the war. The capture of Atlanta convinced enough Americans in the

United States that Lincoln knew what he was doing. Lincoln won the Presidential election in a landslide in November 1864, but he did so by tight margins in major states like Pennsylvania and New York.

General Sherman then prepared for a more daring victory - a march through the heart of Georgia to Savannah on the Atlantic Ocean. Before he did so, he ordered civilians evacuated from Atlanta. He feared Confederate sympathizers might sabotage his base of operations.

Atlantans condemned Sherman's decision to clear out the city. In response to a petition from Atlanta's mayor asking him to revoke the evacuation order, Sherman famously replied, "You cannot qualify war in harsher terms than I will. War is cruelty, and you cannot refine it: and those who brought war into our

Country deserve all the curses and maledictions a people can pour out."

Before advancing deep into Georgia, Sherman notified Grant of his plan. In early October, Sherman telegrammed that he aimed for the "utter destruction" of all roads and houses to cripple the military resources available to the rebels. "I can make the march and make Georgia howl," explained Sherman.

In mid-November, Sherman pulled out of Atlanta with 62,000 troops. He faced little opposition from enemy units. The Union Army cut a 60-mile-wide path of devastation along a 250-mile march to Savannah, Georgia, on the Atlantic coast. The heart of the Confederacy had been gutted.

On December 21, 1864, General Sherman arrived at Savannah. Rather than risk damage to the city, the residents surrendered without a fight. Sherman offered the city to President Lincoln as a Christmas present.

Did you know?

- Gen. William T. Sherman was appointed the first president of the Louisiana State Seminary of Learning and Military Academy in 1859. He taught engineering and military tactics at the school. He resigned when Louisiana seceded. The school later became Louisiana State University.

- Andrew Johnson, Lincoln's choice for vice-president in 1864, was a United States Senator from Tennessee when the state seceded. Being from staunchly pro-Union eastern Tennessee, Johnson refused to resign from Congress. He was the only member of Congress from a seceded state not to resign.

- Ambrose Bierce became a newspaper editor in California and a nationally famous author. His short story *An Occurrence at Owl Creek Bridge* is widely anthologized in collections of American fiction. Drawing on his wartime experiences, Bierce pioneered realist fiction and horror writing.

- The destruction of Atlanta during Sherman's campaign made the city a symbol of rebuilding the South after the Civil War. In 1860, the Atlanta population stood at 9,554 people, ranking it 99th in size in the United States. Today the city ranks as the eighth-largest metropolitan area in the United States with over 6.1 million people.

- Desperate to break the Union blockade, Confederate engineers developed the first successful submarine. On February 17, 1864, the CSS Hunley torpedoed the USS

Housatonic near Charleston, South Carolina. The CSS Hunley sank on the journey back to port, with all crew lost, either due to the blast weakening the hull or incapacitating the crew.

- Fighting a defensive war, the Confederacy introduced landmines to modern warfare. In 1862, Confederate General Gabriel Rains developed the first mechanical high-explosive landmine, a converted artillery shell, detonated by the pressure of someone stepping on it.

APPOMATTOX COURT HOUSE

Worn down by months of constant combat and stretched by the continued extension of the Union Army around Richmond and nearby Petersburg, the Confederates defending the rebel capital had run out of options. With supplies low and reinforcements unavailable, General Lee's Army of Northern Virginia could no longer defend the system of trenches over 30 miles long and growing longer.

Confederate President Jefferson Davis was at church when a messenger rushed up with a sealed envelope. Inside was a telegram from General Lee: "I advise that all preparation be made for leaving Richmond tonight." It was April 2, 1865. And Grant's army had finally broken through Lee's defensive positions, threatening Lee's main supply line and retreat route.

The Confederate government scrambled to evacuate. Lee's army followed. Every minute wasted risked the survival of the Confederacy.

Learning that Lee had largely emptied the trenches around Richmond and Petersburg, Grant raced to prevent Lee's army from achieving one of two destinations. Lee could take his men westward to the Appalachian Mountains to engage in a guerilla war. Or, Lee could escape southward to combine with the Army of Tennessee, a force again under the command of General Joseph Johnston. Grant ordered his men to chase down Lee's rebels.

Two days after the Confederate evacuation of Richmond, President Lincoln arrived in the city. Despite aides warning him about the dangers of entering the former rebel capital, Lincoln wanted to see the city for which so many Americans gave their lives. He stepped off a warship with his son Tad and strolled the streets with a small guard of sailors. Immediately, liberated African Americans surrounded Lincoln, shaking his hand and thanking him for ending enslavement. Lincoln spent the day surveying the city before heading back to Washington, D.C.

Pushing his men hard over the next week, Grant finally trapped Lee's exhausted rebels near a village called Appomattox Court House. On April 9, 1865, Lee met with Grant under a flag of truce to surrender the Army of Northern Virginia.

When news of the surrender reached Washington, D.C., the next day, crowds gathered to cheer President Lincoln. A band gathered at the White House. Lincoln asked the musicians to play "Dixie," the unofficial anthem of the Confederate States. Lincoln joked, "I have always thought 'Dixie' one of the best tunes I have ever heard. Our adversaries over the way attempted to appropriate it, but I insisted yesterday that we fairly captured it."

With the largest Confederate Army now defeated, the remaining rebel forces struggled to continue the fight. Time was not on their side.

Union General William T. Sherman, after capturing Savannah, Georgia, near Christmas 1864, had moved his troops northward through South Carolina in an effort to join up, eventually, with Grant's army at Richmond. General Joseph Johnston's Confederates shadowed Sherman's advancing soldiers looking for attempts to slow them down. Receiving news of Lee's surrender, Johnston recognized the pointlessness of continuing the fight. So did his men. Johnson's army of 22,000 soldiers slowly melted away as 8,000 deserters abandoned their units to go home. Johnston met with Sherman to surrender his army of Southerners on April 26, 1865.

Both Grant and Sherman offered leniency to the rebel soldiers. If the southern troops handed over their firearms and did not attempt to rejoin the fighting, they could return home and never face prosecution for treason against the United States. Confederate officers were permitted to keep their sidearms and their horses.

Other, smaller Confederate armies and garrisons surrendered over the next month. The slow unraveling of the Confederacy between April and June 1865 allowed chaos to reign over the southern countryside. The Confederate government never formally surrendered. It had simply evaporated as officials and politicians scattered. Union cavalry captured Confederate

President Jefferson Davis on May 10, 1865, near Irwinville, Georgia.

The last Confederate Army to furl its flag was in Texas. When the Union military seized the Mississippi River in 1863, the states of Texas, Arkansas, and most of Louisiana were cut off from the rest of the Confederacy. This theater of the war, known as the Trans-Mississippi Theater, was under the command of the Confederate General Edmund Kirby Smith. He surrendered his forces at Galveston, Texas, on June 2, 1865.

The Civil War was over.

News of these surrenders should have sparked joyous celebrations across the United States. Certainly, residents of the northern states erupted in revelry on hearing of Lee's surrender at Appomattox.

But the mood quickly turned dark. Americans fell into deep mourning on news that President Lincoln had been shot in the back of the head while watching a play at Ford's Theatre in Washington, D.C., on the evening of April 14, 1865. He died the next morning.

Lincoln had been killed as part of a conspiracy hatched by Confederate sympathizer John Wilkes Booth. He was the first United States president ever assassinated. A well-known actor familiar with Ford's Theatre, Booth planned to topple the United States government, plunging the northern states into chaos in order to rescue the collapsing Confederacy.

Booth worked independently of the Confederate military or government. But he found a number of men around Washington, D.C., willing to help him. After an earlier plan to kidnap the President failed, Booth focused on killing him, then fleeing into the Confederacy. He also directed his circle of co-conspirators to assassinate other key members of Lincoln's administration: Secretary of State William Seward and Vice-President Andrew Johnson.

Booth had likely hoped to kill two persons the night he shot Lincoln. General Grant had turned down an invitation to join the President and First Lady, Mary Todd Lincoln. Grant's wife disliked Mrs. Lincoln and refused to attend. When Booth shot Lincoln, the actor leaped from the viewing balcony where the Lincolns sat onto the stage, breaking a leg. He shouted, "Sic semper tyrannis!" The Latin phrase means, "Thus always to tyrants." This was the state motto of Virginia.

Near the same moment a man named Lewis Powell, a Confederate soldier who worked among partisans in northern Virginia and Maryland, entered the home of William Seward. The Secretary of State was bedridden after a recent carriage accident. Pretending to deliver medicine, Powell pushed aside Seward's family members, knifed a guard, and began stabbing Seward around his throat and head several times before fleeing. The metal splint around Seward's jaw, placed there as part of his recovery, blocked some of the knife thrusts, likely saving his life.

The conspirator assigned the task of killing Vice-President Johnson failed to act.

An intense manhunt rounded up the conspirators over the next several days. Union soldiers cornered Booth in a tobacco barn in northern Virginia. They set the barn on fire to flush him out. One soldier fired at a movement inside, killing Booth.

Overall, eight conspirators were captured and tried by a military court for Lincoln's murder. Four were found guilty and hanged in July 1865. The other four were sentenced to life imprisonment.

In the meantime, Lincoln's funeral train of nine railroad cars had carried the casket containing the President on a tour of the United States. The train traveled some 1,700 miles on a winding route so Americans could see and mourn the dead Commander-in-Chief who had won the Civil War. About 25 million Americans paid their respects during the train's journey to Springfield, Illinois, Lincoln's final resting place.

Did you know?

- The McLean House at Appomattox was owned by Wilmer McLean and his wife Virginia. They had moved to the remote village to get away from the war in northern Virginia after the Confederates and Federals partly fought the Battle of Bull Run on their farm in 1861.

- Ely Parker, a lieutenant colonel on Union General Grant's staff, was born a Seneca, a Native American people in New York. Parker drafted the surrender document signed by Confederate General Lee at Appomattox. On seeing Parker, Lee remarked, "I am glad to see one real American here." Parker responded, "We are all Americans, sir."

- The last shot of the Civil War was fired by the commerce raider CSS Shenandoah when the crew fired a warning shot over a whaling vessel near Alaska on June 22, 1865. The Confederate sailors surrendered their ship at Liverpool in Great Britain on November 6, 1865, the last rebels to surrender.

- Confederate General Joseph Johnston deeply respected Union General William T. Sherman. They became close friends. Johnston even served as an honorary pallbearer at Sherman's funeral. Despite warnings about the cold and rain, Johnston refused to wear his hat out of respect for Sherman. He caught pneumonia and died shortly after the funeral.

- Many leaders and citizens of the Confederacy feared arrest, imprisonment, and possible execution for their roles in the rebellion. Some white southerners also feared reprisals by their formerly enslaved African Americans. Around 10,000 white southerners fled to Brazil, where they became known as Confederados. Brazil allowed enslavement until 1888.

- Most former Confederates quickly received paroles and eventually pardons, restoring their citizenship to the United States. After his capture, Confederate President Jefferson Davis was imprisoned for two years at Fortress Monroe, Virginia. Federal officials released him fearing that a treason trial might show the legality of secession. In 1978, President Jimmy Carter officially granted Davis a pardon.

RECONSTRUCTION

The disintegration of the Confederacy and the assassination of Lincoln plunged the United States into an uncertain future. How would the defeated southern states be reconstructed and returned to the United States? How far would the United States extend the political rights of African Americans freed from enslavement now that victory had been achieved? Would the formerly enslaved be ensured educational opportunities, social equality, and economic assistance?

President Lincoln, eager to restore the Union as quickly as possible, had emphasized leniency on the seceded states. He had seen too much bloodshed and sought to build a peaceful new future.

A month before his assassination, he spoke at his second inauguration: "With malice toward none; with charity for all; with firmness in the right, as God gives us to see the right, let us strive on to finish the work we are in; to bind up the nation's wounds; to care for him who shall have borne the battle, and for his widow, and his orphan - to do all which may achieve and cherish a just and lasting peace among ourselves, and with all nations."

Lincoln looked to aid the enslaved and the defeated rebels left destitute by the war. In March 1865, he had pushed through Congress an act creating the Bureau of Refugees, Freedmen, and Abandoned Lands.

The agency, known simply as the Freedmen's Bureau, distributed food and other supplies to the poor in the South, white and black. But critics focused increasingly on the agency's role in working with African Americans. Officials in the organization helped formerly enslaved African Americans, often illiterate, to negotiate work contracts with white landowners, many of whom had been enslavers. These contracts usually involved sharecropping, meaning that laborers paid rent by handing over a share of the crop raised on the land they rented. Primarily active between June 1865 and December 1868, the Freedmen's Bureau was not abolished until 1872.

Lincoln's death put Andrew Johnson in the White House. Although a Unionist, Johnson questioned efforts to achieve racial equality. He was, after all, a white Southerner from Tennessee raised in a pro-slavery society. Johnson pardoned numerous Confederate leaders. As a poor man who never attended school, the President taught himself to read and write. Now in the White House, he enjoyed having wealthy plantation owners and rebel leaders plead with him for pardons.

Johnson's approach to reconstructing the former Confederacy angered many northerners. Unionists and African Americans in the South also complained. Under the lenient terms of surrender, voters across the defeated Confederacy elected many former rebel officers and politicians to the United States Congress.

The state legislatures of the South also passed Black Codes, a range of laws that largely restored the conditions of enslavement of African Americans in all but name. The ratification of the Thirteenth Amendment in December 1865 finally prohibited enslavement throughout the United States. But the Black Codes tried to restore racial division. Violent massacres of African Americans occurred in New Orleans and Memphis in 1866.

Even after four bloody years of warfare, white southerners remained as defiant as ever. It seemed that the Union victory achieved on the battlefield in 1865 had become an empty victory by 1866.

The Republican Party, especially a vocal faction known as the Radical Republicans, became furious. They condemned the ease with which white Southerners elected former Confederates. They protested the wave of violence unleashed by the ex-rebels against liberated African Americans.

The formerly enslaved loyally voted Republican, recognizing that the party of Abraham Lincoln had destroyed the practice of slavery. Radical Republicans aimed to protect these African Americans, both to preserve their rights and to rescue a key voting block that could keep the Republican Party in power.

The Radical Republicans responded by asserting their majority in Congress to restrict President Johnson and his program known as Presidential Reconstruction. They now launched what was called Congressional Reconstruction. Overriding attempts by Johnson to block, or veto, the acts passed by Congress, the House of Representatives and Senate backed laws strengthening the Freedmen's Bureau and affirming African Americans' civil rights.

Particularly important was the Reconstruction Act of 1867. The law outlined the terms former Confederate states had to meet before receiving readmission to the United States. Ten of the 11 rebel states were subject to the Act. Only Tennessee, with a large Unionist population in the eastern part of the state who remained loyal throughout the Civil War, was exempt. Tennessee, in July 1866, was the first former Confederate state fully restored to the Union.

The Act required the former Confederate states to ratify state constitutions that recognized the right of all men to vote regardless of race. Over 700,000 African Americans registered to vote across the South, with black voters forming a majority of the electorate in Alabama, Florida, Louisiana, Mississippi, and South Carolina, states where many ex-Confederates still faced voting restrictions due to their disloyalty.

Under the Act, these states also had to ratify the Fourteenth Amendment to the United States Constitution. The Amendment guaranteed the citizenship rights of all Americans and was ratified in 1868. It stated, "No state shall make or enforce any law which shall abridge the privileges or immunities of citizens of the United States; nor shall any state deprive any person of life, liberty, or property, without due process of law; nor deny to any person within its jurisdiction the equal protection of the laws." Ever since the Amendment has served as the foundation of Americans' civil rights.

To oversee the reconstruction of the southern states into a more equitable society, Congress divided the ten states subject to the Act into five military districts. In a sense, these states were now under martial law with Union troops protecting Republican politicians and their supporters.

Radical Republicans also restrained President Johnson from interfering with Congress's efforts to reform the defeated Confederate states. Congress passed the Tenure of Office Act in March 1867, prohibiting the President from removing federal officials appointed with approval by the United States Senate without also seeking approval for their removal.

When President Johnson removed Secretary of War William Stanton without consent, Congress moved to impeach, or remove, Johnson from the presidency on charges of acting illegally. Johnson became the first president ever to face an impeachment trial. By one vote, Johnson was acquitted of the charges against him, but he remained a weakened president.

The Republican Party rallied support for General Ulysses S. Grant to run for president in 1868. A war hero, Grant would serve two terms, guiding the country through Reconstruction until he left office in 1877.

Most white southerners who had fought in the rebellion resisted all efforts to empower African Americans with the vote and to grant them access to public transit, schools, restaurants, and other facilities based on racial equality.

In the late 1860s, they joined paramilitary groups like the Knights of the White Camellia in Louisiana or the Red Shirts in South Carolina. These vigilante organizations were often organized along military lines mimicking their former rebel units. Wearing disguises to hide their identities, these terrorists unleashed a wave of violence, including whippings, murders, and arson attacks, on African Americans and any advocates of racial equality, including a few former Confederate leaders who called for social reform.

The violence became known in the northern press as Ku Kluxism. This name came from the most prominent terrorist organization emerging across the former Confederacy, the Ku Klux Klan. Founded in Tennessee in December 1865, the Klan named former Confederate General Nathan Bedford Forrest as the leader, giving him the title Grand Wizard.

Forrest was notorious for having led a Confederate force that captured Fort Pillow near Memphis, Tennessee, in April 1864. African American soldiers defended the fort. Breaching the walls, Forrest's rebels murdered most of these Union troops when they tried to surrender.

Congressional Reconstruction succeeded in briefly creating more racially equal societies in the South despite hostility from many whites. African Americans rode on public transit, attended integrated schools, gained election, and ate at restaurants with whites, among other advances. Alabama, Arkansas, Florida, Georgia, Louisiana, North Carolina, and South Carolina rejoined the Union in 1868. But Georgia's politicians immediately kicked out of the legislature all African Americans, leading Congress to reimpose military rule.

Texas, Mississippi, and Virginia rejoined the Union in 1870. Georgia too finally reapplied for admission in 1870, becoming the last state permanently reincorporated into the United States.

The violence across the defeated Confederacy became so great that Congress passed the Enforcement Acts during 1870 and 1871, popularly known as the Ku Klux Klan Acts. These Acts banned persons from forming groups or wearing disguises with the intent of denying any American citizens of their rights. Congress also placed elections to federal offices, like the Presidency or Congress, under the supervision of the federal courts and US marshals. Finally, the Acts authorized the President to use federal troops to combat groups like the Ku Klux Klan.

The effort to suppress terrorist groups across the South aimed to ensure respect for African Americans' rights under the Fourteenth Amendment, and now the Fifteenth Amendment, which had been ratified in 1870. The new Amendment guaranteed all citizens, regardless of race, the right to vote.

But the violence continued to rage across the former Confederacy. White supremacists especially targeted any African Americans attempting to vote. Despite the restoration of all the former Confederate states to the Union by 1870, federal troops remained in several to protect African Americans and, generally, Republicans, all of whom faced vicious attacks by white terrorists.

Albion Tourgee, a northerner working in North Carolina to aid African Americans, witnessed the cruelty of white vigilantes' intent on undermining efforts to reconstruct race relations in the South. He observed, "There was no good man, no honest man, no Christian man of the South who for an instant claimed that it was right to kill, maim, beat, wound and ill-treat the black man, either in his old or his new estate." A few may have. But white southerners preferred to see themselves as caretakers rather than abusers of African American.

Tourgee easily explained this contradiction between white Southerners' views on violence and their views on race. The white southerner "did not regard these acts as done to another *man*, a compeer, but only as acts of cruelty to an inferior so infinitely removed from himself as to forbid any comparison of rights or feelings."

In Louisiana, for example, William Pitt Kellogg, the Republican governor, condemned the ongoing violence against African Americans and their white allies. In 1873, he lamented, "Under a system of law according equal political justice to all, securing the individual rights of every person, without regard to nationality, color, race or religion, it is to be regretted that there is a disposition to prevent the newly enfranchised citizen from freely exercising his right to vote." The aim was clear. The violence was "calculated to engender antagonism between capital and labor," concluded the governor.

So bad were conditions in Louisiana that in September 1874 an armed insurrection occurred against Governor Kellogg. A pitched battle occurred between white supremacist groups and the state militia in New Orleans, briefly overthrowing Kellogg. President Grant rushed federal troops to Louisiana to restore Kellogg's government. Despite this, Louisiana continued to function with two governments, one run by Republicans and another run by Democrats.

The continuing violence across the South exhausted northern supporters of reform. Reconstruction had become a war of attrition between the terrorist groups looking to reverse advances in African Americans' voting and civil rights and northern voters who had sought to make a more perfect Union after the Confederacy's surrender.

Events in 1870 led even strong supporters of Reconstruction to lose commitment to the reform efforts. A six-year-long economic depression, sparked by the Panic of 1873, distracted Americans from reconstructing the South. Northern investors lost their money, usually due to railroad companies that went bankrupt, and workers struggled to find jobs.

Americans' trust in President Grant eroded as well. During his reelection campaign in 1872, a newspaper broke the Credit Mobilier scandal. Credit Mobilier was a construction company founded by the Union Pacific Railroad, an operator of the transcontinental railroad linking the eastern United States to California. The company overbilled the US government and bribed politicians and government officials in Washington, D.C., to ease regulations restricting the railroad.

The controversy over the results of the 1876 Presidential election marked the end of Reconstruction. The Democratic candidate, Samuel Tilden, received a majority, nearly 51%, of the popular vote. But neither he nor his Republican challenger, Rutherford B. Hayes, had won the Electoral College.

Disputes over the votes in Louisiana, Florida, and South Carolina, which had each submitted two different totals showing two different winners, led Congress to establish a committee to review these results. The Republican majority on the committee voted to recognize the votes having Hayes the winner. This gave him a one-vote win in the Electoral College even though he received just under 48% of the national popular vote.

A secret deal, known as the Compromise of 1877, brokered the election to Hayes. Democrats from the three southern states agreed not to protest the committee's decision. In return, Republicans promised that Hayes, as president, would withdraw the remaining federal troops from the South. No longer would Republicans so actively enforce racial equality and voting protections.

When Hayes took the oath of office to become president in 1877, Reconstruction ended. The Union had won the Civil War by bleeding the rebel armies to the point of collapse, but the defeated Confederates had outlasted the Radical Republican reformers who had hoped to ensure the civil rights of the African Americans liberated from enslavement.

Did you know?

- Secretary of State William Seward continued to serve under President Andrew Johnson after recovering from the assassination attempt in 1865. In October 1867, Seward negotiated the purchase of Alaska by the United States from Russia, which claimed the territory, for just over $7 million. Many Americans ridiculed the acquisition of such a cold, barren land, labeling the deal "Seward's Folly."

- Congress, in 1862, authorized the construction of a transcontinental railroad to link California to the rest of the United States. The Central Pacific Railroad was built eastward from Sacramento, California, and the Union Pacific Railroad was built westward from Omaha, Nebraska. The railroad line, nearly 2,000 miles long, was completed on May 10, 1869, at Promontory, Utah.

- Under President Grant, General Philip Sheridan received orders to force Native Americans on the Great Plains onto reservations, lands designated by the federal government. Sheridan applied tactics he learned during the Civil War. He attacked during the winter when Native Americans camped. He also attacked their main source of food and clothing by encouraging the killing of buffalo.

- Faced with worsening discrimination and violence, around 20,000 African Americans, mostly from Mississippi, Louisiana, and Texas, moved to Kansas from 1879–1881. They were called Exodusters. A Kansas law passed in 1879 allowed racial segregation of schools. A challenge to this law in 1954 led to the US Supreme Court's *Brown v. Board of*

Education of Topeka, Kansas decision, banning school segregation in the United States.

- A wave of new inventions began to change American society during the 1870s. Alexander Graham Bell invented the telephone. Thomas Edison perfected the electric light bulb and discovered a way of recording sound on a device called the phonograph. By the 20th century, these new technologies would become increasingly common in Americans' homes.

- Harriet Beecher Stowe, author of *Uncle Tom's Cabin*, purchased property on the St. Johns River near Jacksonville, Florida, in the late 1860s. Stowe spent the winters in Florida to enjoy the warm weather. Her writings about Florida, published as *Palmetto Leaves* in 1873, are credited with helping to turn the former Confederate state into a popular vacation destination.

CONCLUSION

For four long years, a divided United States warred. Over 600,000 Northerners and Southerners died to resolve two key questions about the future of the country that had haunted Americans ever since their ancestors declared independence in 1776.

First, the conflict answered the question of African Americans' enslavement. All Americans would be free. Slavery would never again exist in the United States.

Second, the war resolved the debate about the authority of states over the power of the federal government. The United States was a nation, not a loose association of states that could easily leave the Union.

But the war left incomplete the issue of ensuring racial equality and economic opportunity for African Americans who had endured centuries of enslavement at the hands of white enslavers in the South.

Most white Southerners, whether they owned humans or not, continued to resist change. They surrendered the Confederacy, but they would not surrender white supremacy. Many white northerners agreed, ultimately tiring of efforts by the United States government to improve race relations during Reconstruction.

This left deep national wounds that refused to heal, wounds that reopened during more bloody battles for civil rights in the 20th century.

With the end of Reconstruction, white northerners and white southerners set aside old animosities. Henry Grady, the editor of the *Atlanta Constitution* newspaper, became a spokesperson for a "New South." He celebrated the end of slavery and welcomed investment from northerners.

Grady, like most people in the former Confederacy, refused to accept blame for the war or slavery. In one speech, Grady famously proclaimed to a room full of northerner businessmen, "The South has nothing for which to apologize. She believes that the late struggle between the States was war and not rebellion; revolution and not conspiracy, and that her convictions were as honest as yours."

During the late 19th and early 20th century, white southerners generally reimagined the Confederacy as a Lost Cause. The Lost Cause myth taught generations of white Southerners, and even white Northerners, that the rebellion was a brave defense of homes, not a defense of the buying and selling of human beings. Secession was a legal right according to the myth. Confederates were said to have fought for independence even though they knew their effort was doomed because of northern industrial might.

Across the South, from the 1880s through the 1920s, thousands of monuments to Confederate soldiers, generals, and politicians were erected. Most of these were funded by an organization called the United Daughters of the Confederacy. The group also wrote textbooks that taught the Lost Cause myth to southern children into the mid-20th century.

Enslavement of human beings was largely forgotten as a reason for the Civil War by the late 19th century. Worse, African Americans were said to have stayed loyal to their owners throughout the conflict and were supposedly treated well by their enslavers. This myth justified white supremacy and the denial of African Americans' rights won by the sacrifice of so many lives during the Civil War.

Through acceptance of the Lost Cause myth, white Northerners and white Southerners united over shared racism. When the United States plunged into the Spanish-American War in 1898, the country marched as a united nation. A former Confederate general named Joseph Wheeler even led troops as a United States general during this conflict. The future president Theodore Roosevelt served as a lieutenant colonel under Wheeler's command.

African Americans, 90% of whom lived in the South in the late 19th century, would struggle to regain the rights they fleetingly enjoyed during Reconstruction. Segregation laws, also called Jim Crow laws, and an acceptance of violence repressed African Americans across the former Confederacy from the 1880s through the 1960s. Few were allowed to vote. Conditions became so bad that thousands began to flee to northern cities where racism was less intense.

This flight by African Americans, known as the Great Migration, made the issue of civil rights for people of color a national issue rather than a matter largely rooted in the former Confederacy. Through organizations like the National Association for the Advancement of Colored People, founded in New York in 1909, African Americans began lawsuits and protests to enforce protections guaranteed by the Fourteenth and Fifteenth Amendments and to pressure government officials to enforce laws like the Ku Klux Klan Acts.

By the 1940s, African Americans advocated mass public protests, launching the modern Civil Rights Movement. This movement culminated in the 1960s, during centennial memorials to the Civil War.

Protesters like Martin Luther King, Jr., noted that the Civil Rights Movement was an effort to complete the job started by the Civil War. In his "I Have a Dream" Speech in front of the Lincoln Memorial in 1963, King celebrated the Emancipation Proclamation ending enslavement. He then announced that African Americans remained "sadly crippled by the manacles of segregation and the chains of discrimination."

King dreamed of a day when the "sons of former slaves and the sons of former slave owners will be able to sit down together at the table of brotherhood."

Congress answered King's call and those of other civil rights activists by passing the Civil Rights Act of 1964 and the Voting Rights Act of 1965. African Americans, under the 1964 legislation, gained the right to enjoy restaurants, transit systems, hotels, and other businesses serving the public by ending local and state laws enforcing racial segregation. The 1965 law protected African Americans' right to vote.

What historians have come to call the Second Reconstruction of the 1950s and 1960s fulfilled the promises of the First Reconstruction of the 1860s and 1870s.

But the debates over race and rights that led to the Civil War remain with Americans today as the nation continues to confront discrimination based on skin color.

Made in United States
Orlando, FL
13 December 2024

55584895R00085